P9-DWS-468

HAUNTED CANADA 8

MORE CHILLING TRUE TALES

HAUNTED CANADA 8

MORE CHILLING TRUE TALES

JOEL A.
SUTHERLAND

Illustrations by
Mark Savona

Scholastic Canada Ltd.
Toronto New York London Auckland Sydney
Mexico City New Delhi Hong Kong Buenos Aires

Scholastic Canada Ltd.
604 King Street West, Toronto, Ontario M5V 1E1, Canada

Scholastic Inc.
557 Broadway, New York, NY 10012, USA

Scholastic Australia Pty Limited
PO Box 579, Gosford, NSW 2250, Australia

Scholastic New Zealand Limited
Private Bag 94407, Botany, Manukau 2163, New Zealand

Scholastic Children's Books
Euston House, 24 Eversholt Street, London NW1 1DB, UK

www.scholastic.ca

Library and Archives Canada Cataloguing in Publication

Sutherland, Joel A., 1980-, author
Haunted Canada 8 : more chilling true tales / Joel A. Sutherland ;
illustrated by Mark Savona.

Issued in print and electronic formats.
ISBN 978-1-4431-4883-2 (softcover).--ISBN 978-1-4431-4888-7 (ebook)

1. Ghosts--Canada--Juvenile literature. 2. Haunted places--
Canada--Juvenile literature. I. Savona, Mark, illustrator II. Title.
III. Title: Haunted Canada eight.

BF1472.C3S985 2018   j133.10971   C2017-906941-1
                                                C2017-906942-X

Cover credits:
Photo © abdreiuc88/Fotolia.

Illustrations by Mark Savona.

Text copyright © 2018 by Joel A. Sutherland.
Illustrations copyright © 2018 by Scholastic Canada Ltd.
All rights reserved.
No part of this publication may be reproduced or stored in a retrieval system, or
transmitted in any form or by any means, electronic, mechanical, recording, or
otherwise, without written permission of the publisher, Scholastic Canada Ltd.,
604 King Street West, Toronto, Ontario M5V 1E1, Canada. In the case of photo-
copying or other reprographic copying, a licence must be obtained from Access
Copyright (Canadian Copyright Licensing Agency), 56 Wellesley Street West,
Suite 320, Toronto, Ontario M5S 2S3 (1-800-893-5777).

7 6 5 4 3 2   Printed in Canada   139   18 19 20 21 22

RECYCLED
Paper made from
recycled material
FSC® C103567

*In memory of Murphy,
forever my good dog.*

INTRODUCTION

When I'm writing a new volume of the Haunted Canada series, it's hard for me to predict which stories will be the ones that stand out as the most terrifying, creepy or intense.

Take, for example, the story I wrote about a museum display of antique dolls. I'm willing to bet that you just shivered uncontrollably simply by picturing a display of antique dolls! I didn't expect that story from *Haunted Canada 4*, titled "Dead-Eyed Dolls," to be one of the scariest in that volume, but most readers have reported that it freaked them out more than any other.

Clearly, there's something unnerving about dolls. So I was thrilled to learn about Lizzie, a doll from Niagara-on-the-Lake, and I wrote about her in *Haunted Canada 6*.

And now, lucky for you (or unfortunately for you, depending on your outlook), I've discovered one of the meanest, most frightening dolls in the country. Her name is Mandy, and her story appears in this book. I have a feeling you'll find "Mandy Lives" one of the most memorable stories in *Haunted Canada 8*.

Or perhaps you'll be more scared by the thought of seeing floating red eyes outside your bedroom window, as in "Secret Room," or by living with a poltergeist in your attic, as in "The Etobicoke Poltergeist," or by swimming with a corpse, as in "The Body in the Brook," or by playing in a park that was once a cemetery, as in "Skeleton Park."

Then again, who knows? Perhaps you'll think one of the other stories in this volume is the scariest. That's part of the fun of spooky stories. Fear is subjective. What scares me might not scare you, and vice versa.

There's only one way to find out which stories will really get under your skin and keep you up at night: read on.

But there's one thing I think we can all agree on. Dolls are terrifying.

Don't say I didn't warn you.

Frightfully yours,

THE ETOBICOKE POLTERGEIST

Toronto, Ontario

Reverend Tom Bartlett of the Star of Progress Spiritualist Church climbed the stairs to the attic alone. If his pulse was racing and his knees were shaking, he could hardly be blamed. He was preparing to perform an exorcism.

The house on Prince Edward Drive South was surrounded by bushes and trees, giving it a closed-in feeling on an otherwise bright and cheery street in Etobicoke, a suburb in Toronto's west end. It was built shortly before Park Lawn Cemetery, which opened nearby in 1892 and is home to more than 22,000 graves. The home was originally a farmhouse before the subdivision sprung up around it.

It was early May of 1968 and Albert Cracknell and his wife rented the house for the sum of 250 dollars a month. They lived on the main floor with their ten-year-old daughter, Shirley, while the Cracknells' twenty-seven-year-old daughter, Carol Hawkins, lived in the second-floor apartment with her husband, Roy, and their two daughters, Sherry and Trudy. Carol and Roy's nine-month-old son, Stephen, was in the hospital, which understandably placed a lot of stress on the family. Otherwise, everyone was happy. The house was full, but it was also quite large, and everyone was comfortable living together. They had no plans to move any time soon and had nothing but pleasant feelings for the house.

That all changed very quickly. It was a warm night when Carol was awoken by the sound of feet pounding across the attic floor above her head. First *thump, thump, thump* from left to right, then *thump, thump, thump* from right to left. This commotion was followed by piercing, screeching laughter. Although the heavy footsteps and hysterical laughter came from the attic, both were so loud that it sounded to Carol as if an old woman was right beside her in the bedroom.

She woke her husband and they both listened in blind terror as the running and laughing continued through the night. When they finally built up the courage to get out of bed and check on their daughters, who were asleep in the next room, the noises stopped abruptly. Like the girls, Carol's parents and sister had also slept through the chaos, perhaps because their bedrooms were farther away, on the main floor.

Early the next morning, the family searched the attic thoroughly but couldn't find any sign that anything unusual had taken place up there through the night, nor any explanation for what had created the sounds. Exhausted, Carol went back to bed. Shortly after her head hit the pillow and she closed her eyes, she felt as if someone was leaning over her in the bed. She opened her eyes and found that the room was empty, but then a sudden chill passed through her body as if a ghost had just flown through her.

That night, the same thumps and laughter broke Carol and Roy's sleep. Whoever was moving about and cackling in the attic did so from 2 a.m. until the sun came up. Desperately needing a break, the Hawkinses spent the following night at a friend's house. But when they returned home, they had the worst night yet.

This time, the noises started at 12:30 a.m., and the footsteps were followed not by laughter, but by a high-pitched screech that sounded like nails dragging across a chalkboard. Roy, at his wits' end, shouted at whatever was disrupting their sleep to keep quiet and leave them alone. Shockingly, his desperate command worked — for a short while, anyway.

At 4 a.m. they were awoken by the poltergeist once more. Their cat, Fluffy, left their bedroom and walked past the stairs to the attic, out of sight of the married couple. Just then they heard a loud thump and Fluffy meowed in pain as if she had been kicked. This was followed by the same high-pitched screech the ghost had made earlier in the night, which finally gave way to the most ominous and evil-sounding deep-throated laughter they'd ever heard.

Carol thought Fluffy must be dead. Roy forced himself

The house on Prince Edward Drive South

out of bed and found the cat in the hallway. Her fur was standing straight up as if she'd received an electric shock, and she was leaning against the wall for support. Her wide eyes were glued to the attic door at the top of the stairs.

The next afternoon, Carol heard the footsteps again, marking the first time the poltergeist was active during broad daylight. But now there was also an unusual brown light filtering out beneath the attic door. Scared for her life,

Carol called a neighbour, Ron Leyzack, who rushed over and searched the attic . . . but found it empty.

Word of the poltergeist spread up and down the street, and one of the neighbours called the *Toronto Telegram.* Two reporters, John Downing and John Gault, arrived and the family welcomed them in. They searched the attic but found nothing out of the ordinary. They interviewed the family and believed their story. Since nothing lined up, the journalists asked if they could spend the night. Carol, for one, was relieved to have some extra company in the house as the sun was setting. Downing and Gault sprinkled flour across the attic floor to capture the footprints of the perpetrator, prints that could be used in identifying the culprit. Satisfied with the plan, everyone went to bed.

They didn't sleep long. At 3:30 a.m. the footsteps thundered overhead. The cat howled and shook in fear. The reporters rushed upstairs, threw open the attic door and turned on the lights, but the attic was empty. The flour was completely undisturbed. There was no explanation for what had happened. Downing and Gault, both skeptics, were starting to believe in ghosts.

The next day, Carol called Reverend Tom Bartlett. The activity had gone far beyond tolerable levels and Carol couldn't take it any longer. Something needed to be done about it, and it needed to be done as soon as possible. The rest of the household agreed completely.

The reverend loved a good challenge, and the poltergeist that had terrorized the family in the old Toronto home certainly fit the bill. Bartlett stopped at the top of the stairs and closed the door behind him, preventing anything — if there was anything — from escaping. Closing the door also trapped him in the attic, but he tried not to think about that. Instead he took in his surroundings.

It was dusk, and the attic was dark and gloomy. The air was still and musty. Cobwebs and dust covered almost every surface. Bartlett noted that there weren't any footprints in the flour. The room was silent.

Bartlett waited a few minutes, alone with his thoughts in the darkness. Nothing happened. His nerves grew taut. The waiting was playing havoc with his mind. He willed the poltergeist to appear.

And then it did. An oval-shaped light with an unusual brownish hue appeared to his left. It looked like a giant, glowing cocoon. Relying upon his knowledge and intuition, Bartlett felt that the spirit was female, that she was ill and that her mind had been heading down a dark path for years. More than anything, he knew that she was obsessed with the house, and was perhaps angry at the people who now lived in it.

Bartlett's wife, Pat, opened the door to the attic and stepped inside. She saw the brown light as well, and then immediately felt sharp pains in her stomach and chest that were so severe it was like she was being stabbed repeatedly with a long knife. Then a loud thumping sound filled the attic, and the temperature plummeted. The poltergeist was clearly agitated by their presence, and given time, the situation would become dangerous.

Reverend Bartlett began the exorcism.

Throughout the ceremony, Carol and the reporters remained a safe distance away, at the foot of the attic stairs. But after Pat rushed upstairs to join her husband, Carol, Downing and Gault saw the strange light under the door and felt an unearthly chill seep into their bones. A short while later Carol fainted and was unconscious for thirty minutes. When she finally came to, she was relieved to hear that the exorcism had been completed and that the reverend and his wife were confident that would be the last time they'd be disturbed by the poltergeist. They left, but the reporters decided to remain one more night, just to make sure the story was over.

As an added precaution, they tied an intricate series of fishing lines from wall to wall throughout the attic, then affixed tiny bells to the strings. No one could pass through the attic without ringing the bells; even an animal or the wind would set them off.

Night fell, and at 11 p.m. the footsteps, much to the dismay of everyone present, began again. The exorcism, apparently, hadn't worked after all. At 2 a.m. a series of ice-cold waves swept through the entire house, chilling everyone's blood. Downing and Gault estimated that the temperature plummeted from 20 to 5 degrees Celsius. The air became damp and the halls were filled with the pungent smell of rotting apples. Ten-year-old Shirley became hysterical with fear and was taken away to spend the rest of the night at her aunt's house. Carol's mother suffered a nervous breakdown and needed to be sedated. Not once through the long night did a single bell ring in the attic.

With no end to the haunting in sight, the Hawkinses and the Cracknells moved out and found new apartments to rent, never to return to the house on Prince Edward Drive

South. It's unknown whether the poltergeist disturbed the next tenants who moved in, but the Bartletts unearthed some information that might explain who the poltergeist was. An elderly woman used to live in the house, and she was known to be a fortune teller. She grew more and more eccentric in her old age and took to spending most days and nights sitting in the attic, yelling at anyone who passed outside. The neighbours complained about the woman and she was forced by her landlord to move, but she didn't go quietly. She insisted that she wanted her son to move in after she died, but she didn't get her wish. Reverend Bartlett is certain this woman was the poltergeist that ran through the attic, attacked the poor cat, laughed through the night and terrorized an unfortunate family throughout the month of May in 1968.

THE HAUNTED CAMP

Lebret, Saskatchewan

The Boy Scouts huddled close together in a circle around the campfire and listened to Camp Gilwell's caretaker share tales of death and ghosts. The young boys didn't make a peep — they were far too scared and nervous. The only sounds were the crackling fire and the occasional shuffling of an animal from within the woods surrounding them. At least they *hoped* those sounds were created by animals, but their imaginations were beginning to get the better of them.

Orange firelight flickered on the caretaker's face, casting moving shadows around his mouth and eyes. He drew his scary story out, increasing the boys' unease. He pointed at the old, dilapidated house not too far from where they sat — a building that was owned by the camp but rarely

9

used — and revelled in telling his rapt audience that the ghost of Mrs. Seymour had been seen and heard on the second floor of that very building.

Just then one of the boys yelled in fright and jumped to his feet. He pointed at the thick bushes beside the house and said, "There was a woman! And a little dog behind her! I swear, I saw them just run into the trees!"

Everyone followed the boy's shaking finger to Seymour House. The area around the house was searched, but there was no sign that a woman or a dog had been there that night. What had the boy seen? Had he imagined it, or had he actually seen a woman and a dog disappear into the woods? It was a mystery, and the caretaker hated mysteries. Unanswered questions crawled into his mind and refused to leave.

It was late and the boys were tired. More than a few had had their fill of horror stories, although they wouldn't admit that to each other. One by one they made their way to their tents, zipped the flaps closed, and slipped into their sleeping bags.

But the caretaker couldn't sleep. He couldn't even rest. He couldn't stop thinking about the woman and the dog.

Could it have been . . . ? he wondered. Although he was certain he'd find Seymour House as empty and undisturbed inside as it had always been, he had to check. After all, he didn't actually believe in ghosts, so he had nothing to fear.

He would soon find out how wrong he was.

He lit his way with a powerful flashlight and pried open Seymour House's rusty front door. As soon as he stepped inside, the window shutters banged violently, as if the house were angry he'd entered. He slowly, carefully climbed the stairs to the second floor, trying his best to tread lightly so the steps wouldn't creak and making certain not to put any weight on the bannister out of fear that it would snap in half.

When he reached the top step and shone his light around the second floor, he stopped dead in his tracks. Because no one had used the second floor for a long time, there was a thick layer of dust on the floor. There was a trail of footprints — the shape and size of a woman's slippered feet — in the dust, leading from the top of the stairs into an unused bedroom. And beside those tracks were dog prints.

It's true, he thought. *It's all true.*

Without crossing the floor and opening the bedroom door — without even hesitating for a second — the caretaker fled from the house.

The story he'd told the Scouts that night was the sad and tragic history of the first Mrs. Seymour, Helena, and her husband, Dr. Maurice Seymour. In the early 1900s, Dr. Seymour treated tuberculosis patients in the nearby Fort Qu'Appelle Sanatorium, and it's believed that he also treated some patients in the house where he and his wife lived with their two small dogs.

Unfortunately, Mrs. Seymour died at a young age. Rumours spread throughout the area that she might have contracted tuberculosis herself, likely thanks to her proximity to people who were infected.

After some time, the doctor remarried. His new wife was

not an animal lover and hated the two dogs. She insisted that they be put down, but Dr. Seymour refused. Instead, he sent the dogs to a boarding kennel. The second Mrs. Seymour would rather not have had the expense of keeping the dogs in the kennel, but she reluctantly agreed to the arrangement. Dogs don't live long, after all, so Father Time would take care of the problem sooner or later.

But that's not the way things played out. Dr. Seymour died before the dogs, and his widow wasted little time contacting the kennel and having the dogs put down. She didn't want to pay for another day.

And that was too great an affront to Dr. Seymour's late first wife. Almost immediately, her spirit returned, restless and distraught. Very soon after the dogs had been euthanized, the doctor's second wife heard the sound of slippered feet scuffling around on the second floor while she was on the main floor late at night. Light was seen in the upstairs windows, and the shutters rattled and banged as if someone was opening them in a panic. And then came the whistling: *fweet-fweet-fweet!* It was the same sound people make when searching for lost dogs.

Then one night, the second Mrs. Seymour came face to face with the first Mrs. Seymour, pacing around the second floor in her slippers, searching and calling for her dogs.

The ghostly confrontation sent the second Mrs. Seymour straight to her room. She packed a bag and left in the middle of the night, never to return to the house again.

Seymour House was sold to Scouts Canada and became part of Camp Gilwell, where the caretaker enjoyed frightening the campers with tall tales that he soon discovered weren't quite so tall after all. For the ghosts of Mrs. Seymour and her dogs continued to rise in the middle of the night, walking through the campgrounds and around the tents, before disappearing in the house where she'd lived . . . and died.

SKELETON PARK

Kingston, Ontario

It was a gorgeous summer afternoon and a man who lived downtown beside McBurney Park was grilling hot dogs and hamburgers in his backyard. He'd invited his friends over for a barbecue. His dog was digging a hole beside the fence nearest the park but no one paid the canine much attention — the sun was shining, everyone had a cold drink and the conversation was lively. The sounds of children laughing and playing in the park competed with distant lawnmowers and music streaming out of a radio. It was a good day to be alive.

But then the dog ran to the patio table where the man and his friends were sitting down to dinner. It had something in its mouth, and it was wagging its tail proudly. As his friends were taking their first bites of the burgers and hot dogs, the man asked his dog to drop whatever was concealed in its mouth. And then, as happily as if it had just fetched its master's slippers, the dog spat a mouthful of bones on the ground. Bones from a human hand.

Needless to say, the group quickly lost their appetites, and the man put his house up for sale shortly thereafter. Had he known the history of McBurney Park — or, as it's more commonly known, Skeleton Park — he wouldn't have been so surprised that his dog had dug human remains out of the backyard.

The site of the park was originally a cemetery called the Upper Burial Ground, which opened in 1819. Although it was one of Kingston's largest cemeteries, it filled up very quickly when epidemics of typhus and cholera hit the city hard in the 1830s and '40s. It reached capacity in 1864. It didn't take long for the cemetery to fall into terrible shape. Local farmers allowed their livestock to wander through it. Families picnicked and children played in it. And vandals knocked over and broke headstones. The state of the cemetery was so bad by 1893 that the city decided to close it for good and turn the land into a public park. The first step was to transfer the bodies to other locations, but two macabre discoveries were soon made.

First, many of the bodies were only buried thirty centimetres below the surface of the ground, probably in an attempt to bury the infected dead as quickly as possible. For the same reason, authorities found mass graves where corpses had been piled one on top of the other; one such grave even contained eleven bodies.

Second, quite a few coffins were completely empty or

Exhumation of the cemetery in McBurney Park

filled with rocks. In the late 1800s, Kingston was home to a group of grave robbers known as the Resurrectionists, criminals who stole bodies from cemeteries, morgues and funeral parlours and sold them to Queens University medical students for dissection.

The city had removed only a few hundred bodies when the park construction project was shut down. Families were expected to pay for the removal of their dearly departed, but most couldn't afford the expense and the city couldn't cover the entire cost. Then concerns arose that digging up the bodies of people who had died from diseases would spread the infections. In the end, the city decided to move forward with plans to turn the cemetery into a park, even though several thousand corpses were still resting in relative peace in the ground. The remaining headstones were knocked flat and dirt was poured over the area, then covered with grass seed. With so many dead lingering beneath the park, it's little wonder that it's haunted by lost, angry souls.

Roughly two hundred years after the cemetery first opened, two young female students moved into an apartment on Ordnance Street, which borders Skeleton Park. They hadn't heard about the park's reputation nor what it had once been. On the day they moved in, one of the students was returning home from class and was surprised to see row upon row of headstones in what she had thought was a park. They were in terrible shape, many knocked over and crumbling, and the large cemetery was filled with an unnatural grey mist that was oddly localized to that area. It wasn't until she passed by the next day and saw the park that she realized what she'd seen the night before was a ghostly image from the past.

The paranormal activity soon bled into their apartment. They felt unusual chills and the claustrophobic sensation of being trapped whenever they were alone. Whispers cut the silence in empty rooms. A heavy candle centrepiece flew off the kitchen counter and shattered. When one of the students returned from classes one day a heavy set of footsteps charged at her from down the hall. The phantom feet stopped right in front of her, stamped once loudly, then were heard no more. Friends saw scary sights in the apartment, like a couch cushion being pressed down as if by an invisible body, and a hovering shadow that glowed blue and seemed to be watching the living with wicked intent.

Just when things seemed like they couldn't get any worse, they did. Both women started dreaming of an evil man who tried to take control of them while they were asleep. One particularly terrifying night, both women woke up at the same time and rushed to each other's rooms. They met in the hallway — one had heard the other choking and gagging, while the other had heard the sounds of a violent struggle. But neither could recall having been attacked.

They couldn't stay in the apartment alone any longer, so they begged and pleaded with their friends to stay over. Some agreed, but no one could stay long. One friend saw a black shadow drift down the hall toward him in the middle of the night. Another friend saw a couple dressed in old-fashioned clothing standing at the top of the stairs as soon as she walked through the front door, and she promptly turned around and left.

A third friend said she'd try her best to help. She claimed to have some paranormal abilities and had contacted spirits in the past. She'd never set foot in the apartment before and, as fate would have it, that wasn't about to change. The night before she had arranged to visit, she dreamed that she was in the apartment, but she wasn't alone. A tall, intimidating man was with her, and he gave off the same overwhelming sense of evil the two women had felt in their apartment. The friend called to cancel and was able to describe the apartment exactly as it appeared, despite the fact that she had never seen it with her own eyes.

Having tried everything they could think of to deal with the problem, the two women were at a loss. They soon moved out of the haunted apartment and found a new place to live on the other side of the city. And who could blame them? Corpses aren't supposed to rise out of their graves, but around Skeleton Park, the dead rise far too frequently.

THE DROWNED MAN

Quebec City, Quebec

It was meant to be a joyous party, a time to celebrate the recent successes of Atkinson, Usborne & Co., a shipping company that transported lumber from Quebec to England. But when a guest showed up unannounced and uninvited, the party promptly died.

It was the mid-1800s and George Usborne was enjoying the extreme wealth that being one of Quebec's leading lumber barons afforded him and his wife, Mary. They lived in a huge stone mansion named Wolf-field Cottage on St. Louis Road in Cap-Rouge, now part of Quebec City. The mansion was located on one hundred acres of waterfront land that was landscaped with beautiful and sprawling gardens, contained a private park and overlooked the St. Lawrence River.

Originally an English sea captain, Usborne came to Canada in 1820 at the age of twenty-four and immediately joined the shipping business, which eventually led him to the lumber business. In those early days, Usborne was an honest man who ran his business by the book. But the more money he made, the more money he *wanted* to make. And he began conjuring up ways to increase his fortune. He decided that if he were to load the timber on the decks in addition to the hull of his ships, he would be able to transport twice as much lumber in the same amount of time, thereby increasing his profits. This was an incredibly dangerous proposition. During a storm there would be a great risk that the square timbers — which could weigh up to a thousand kilograms each — might slide across the deck, killing anyone unfortunate enough to be in their path, and possibly even capsizing the ship. The men protested, but Usborne had made up his mind and refused to budge on the issue. His ship decks were from then on loaded with lumber.

Before long Usborne's wealth grew rapidly. But then tragedy struck.

The party George and Mary threw to celebrate the success of Atkinson, Usborne & Co. was held in the ballroom of their Cap-Rouge mansion. In attendance were some of the wealthiest people from across the province. The women were dressed in expensive clothes from London, and everyone enjoyed the finest wine from Paris. Following a grand feast of the most elegant and rich cuisine of the day, the revellers took to the dance floor as the band played late into the night.

Suddenly there was a knocking on the riverside ballroom door. Even over the lively music and the merry conversations, it seemed as loud as nearby thunder, and the sound echoed throughout the ballroom. The band stopped playing, the dancers stopped dancing, and every pair of eyes — George's and Mary's included — slowly turned to stare at the door.

But it didn't open.

The couple crossed the dance floor and, after a brief pause, opened the door.

A man stood outside on the doorstep. He was alone. He was also dressed in seaman's clothing. Oddly, he was soaking wet and water was pooling around his feet, but the night sky was clear. Odder still, his head and shoulders were covered in seaweed. It looked like he'd been dragged several kilometres underwater at the bottom of the St. Lawrence before being flung out of the river to the very spot where he stood.

None of the party guests, nor the Usbornes, could move or talk. Everyone stood and stared at the mysterious, ill-looking man in silence.

The man raised his arm and pointed at the dead centre of Usborne's chest. Before Usborne could demand to know what he wanted, the man opened his mouth as if to blame Usborne for some heinous wrongdoing. But although his lips moved furiously, no sound escaped them.

And then, before everyone's eyes, the man vanished into thin air. Usborne looked at the doorstep where the man had stood. There on the ground was the pool of water that had run down the man's body.

Not long after, Usborne was informed that one of his ships had been wrecked the same night that the man had knocked on his door. He and his wife both knew that the man must have been the ghost of one of the seamen who had drowned as a result of Usborne's greed. Two more ships were also wrecked, and Usborne soon went bankrupt. He and his wife remained in Quebec City for several years while Usborne attempted to get his business back up off the ground to no avail. It was a stressful time in their lives, but not only because of their financial situation. The same drowned man who had interrupted the party and looked at Usborne with hatred in his waterlogged eyes appeared in the same spot precisely one year later. Once again he opened his mouth and pointed at Usborne as if to cry out an accusation before disappearing. And he returned every year from that day forward with clocklike precision, even after the Usbornes moved out of their stone mansion and left Cap-Rouge to begin a new life elsewhere. Despite the fact that Usborne moved away, it's said that the ghost of the drowned man has refused to leave Cap-Rouge and can be seen once a year looking lost, angry and utterly dead.

THE HILLTOP GRAVE

Glacier Creek, Yukon

The Frenchman had worked for the mining company at Glacier Creek, near Sixty Mile River, for only one month, but he knew to stay far away from the grave on the hill — especially after nightfall. It was a remote location nearly one hundred kilometres west of Dawson City, the nearest town. If something went wrong — and many, many things went wrong near that cursed grave — help was very far away.

And yet one night the Frenchman stayed out a little later than he had intended before seeking shelter for the evening. It was the final night he spent in the area. Something happened to him between nightfall and 3 a.m., at which point he fled in terror.

At first none of the other miners had any idea what had

happened to make a grown man leave his job in the middle of the night. But then word began to spread that the Frenchman had seen something — well, not something, but someone — flying through the starlit sky. It was the ghost of a man trailing a tattered blanket behind his floating corpse, moonlight reflecting brightly off his pallid skin. No one was surprised by the claim and everyone knew exactly who the spectre was. There was a rumour that when John Stockton, the man buried in the grave on the hill, had died, the ground had been too frozen to dig very deep, so his body had simply been wrapped in a blanket and buried half a metre down.

That might explain why the grave is covered with a mound of large rocks. Since John's body couldn't be buried at the standard depth, rocks might have been placed on top to keep wild animals from digging him up. But others think the rocks serve a different purpose and were placed there to keep John from rising from his grave. If that's true, then the rocks aren't very effective.

Very little is known about John Stockton. He arrived sometime in the early 1900s when the Klondike gold rush was still in full swing and the Yukon was filled with miners and prospectors looking to strike it rich. John filed six claims along the creeks and streams near the land where his grave rests today. He was a solitary man who lived alone in a cabin in the woods and would offer a quick "good morning" to anyone he passed on the trails. Although he was a quiet man in life, he has been anything but in death.

Soon after John died in 1944, his claims were purchased by a new miner who recruited many men and set up a fairly large-scale operation. But unexplainable things started to happen. Bad things. The men quickly became convinced that the site was cursed and that John himself was committed to ensuring no one else got rich off the land he had once owned.

No matter where the men placed their lunches at the beginning of their shifts, they would often return later to find all the food had disappeared. Dry land suddenly and inexplicably turned into mudholes large enough to swallow tractors. If they didn't get stuck in mud, the camp vehicles regularly became inoperable due to parts that went missing for no reason. One day in the early 1980s, a man named Jim Ostrowalker was dismayed to find that one of his backhoe's tires had gone flat, and he had a feeling he knew who was responsible. He walked up the hill, sat down beside the grave and said, "This isn't the kind of help I need, John." By the time he returned to his backhoe, the tire had been fixed and inflated. Ostrowalker was the only person there, and the backhoe had been out of sight for only a few minutes.

One of the most annoying problems to plague mining companies in Glacier Creek was the heavy rain that began at 3 p.m. nearly every working day and forced the operation to grind to a halt. The miners described the phenomenon as being weird and unnatural, and they had a gut feeling John was somehow to blame. The rain seemed to fall only on John's old claims and didn't occur on non-working days.

People felt eyes on their backs and heard feet walking behind them on the trails John once traversed, but when

John Stockton's grave

they turned around no one was there. They also heard John opening and closing doors and cupboards in the camp trailers.

Most, if not all, of the miners who have worked in the area over the years have seen the ghost somewhere in camp. Ostrowalker says he saw John fifty or sixty times in the course of one summer. He'd be hard at work when he'd look up the hill and see John standing beside his grave, silently looking down at the operation and perhaps planning his next disturbance. And his efforts have been successful, regularly sending mining companies farther down Glacier Creek where, the owners are happy to discover, none of the same odd problems follow.

Even though John's desire to have his land remain undisturbed should be abundantly clear, there are still those who attempt to seek him out to get some answers. When author Shirley Jonas travelled to Glacier Creek to research his life, she found it difficult to uncover information. After straightening the rocks of his grave she took a walk along Glacier Creek and then stopped, looked back up the hill and, perhaps overcome by a touch of frustration, said, "What do I have to do to find out more about you, John?"

Unexpectedly, a voice answered: "Leave me alone!"

Shirley spun around and looked for the source of the response, but no one was there. She was alone.

But in reality, she wasn't alone. Not truly. Anyone who travels to Glacier Creek will be shadowed by the ghost of John Stockton.

NEVER EVER COME BACK

Stony Plain, Alberta

It was early in the morning when a staff member at the Stony Plain Multicultural Heritage Centre picked up the phone and immediately heard the nearly unintelligible mutterings of a frantic woman on the other end. It took a long time to figure out that the woman who had called was a local artisan and instructor who had led a class in the building the previous evening. Something had clearly upset her a great deal — the staff member got the impression that the instructor had been attacked by some stranger.

"I'll never ever come back," the instructor said with grave seriousness. The instructor had trouble finding the words to adequately describe what had happened.

She had been attacked in the building by someone who was decidedly dead.

The class had taken place in a room on the main floor that was filled with period furniture, artwork and antiques in order to resemble a settler's cabin. The instructor had a lot of equipment to set up for the class and it took her three trips from her car to bring it all inside. The class went off without a hitch, but things took a dark turn after all the students had left. The woman, now completely alone in the building, was packing up her items when she felt the temperature in the room suddenly plummet. The air became colder and colder, so cold that it felt like she was standing in the middle of a walk-in freezer.

The instructor had a terrible feeling in the pit of her stomach, so she hurriedly finished packing up and hauled everything out to her car as quickly as possible. But as she was dealing with her final load, she felt eyes staring at the back of her neck. Goosebumps spread across her skin and she froze, torn between the desire to turn and look or run and hide.

As bad as the cold and the sensation of being watched were, the next thing she felt was much worse and far more threatening. Somehow an unseen presence got inside her head and demanded that she leave the building immediately. She grabbed her last things and rushed out, pausing only to frantically lock the door but unable to pause long enough to set the alarm.

The next morning she told the staff member on the phone that she was certain she'd been chased from the building by a ghost — a very unfriendly ghost — that had scared the living daylights out of her.

The red-brick building was built in 1925 and originally

served as a schoolhouse. It was due to be demolished in the early 1970s, but a group of concerned citizens banded together and formed the Heritage Agricultural Society to save the building. Little did they know they were also saving the ghosts.

Rebecca Still, who used to be the Multicultural Heritage Centre museum manager, also experienced the hostile presence that sent the instructor running out of the building. She claims that there were many instances where she got a really bad sensation and felt like she had overstayed her welcome. Something wanted her to get out. Sometimes when she was working alone in her office, she looked up and spotted a woman in an old-fashioned dress standing in her doorway, but the woman always disappeared in a heartbeat.

The ghostly woman has company on the property in the form of a man who haunts the Oppertshauser House, which is part of the Multicultural Heritage Centre and stands beside the old schoolhouse. His footsteps can be heard passing over the creaky floorboards and he's been known to knock paintings off walls. Items placed in the second floor closet have been discovered in other parts of the house, or have disappeared forever. Some people have heard his voice from within the house while they walk past outside, and a few other particularly unfortunate souls have seen his face peering out at them from one of the upper windows. A staff photo taken outside in broad daylight revealed an odd bluish-white orb floating inside the house.

Debbie Truckey, who worked there, was alone one

Oppertshauser House

Sunday after working a late shift. She locked up and then passed by the Oppertshauser House. When she looked up at the same window, she saw a man with a high collar staring down at her. Debbie wasted no time deciding how to react; she ran as fast as her legs could carry her.

Running from the Stony Plain Multicultural Heritage Centre isn't uncommon. Some return . . . but others never — *ever* — come back.

FRIGHT AT THE MUSEUM

Ottawa, Ontario

It was summer vacation when Anie and her family visited Ottawa for a little sightseeing. On their very first day in the nation's capital they went to the Canadian Museum of Nature, an imposing gothic building that looks like a castle, located in the south end of downtown. Anie saw on a map that the fourth floor had only one permanent exhibit, so she assumed there wouldn't be much to see, but her curiosity got the better of her and she insisted on checking it out, if only briefly. It was a decision she'd soon regret.

Anie headed to the west wing as soon as she reached the fourth floor, her sister and mother trailing behind her. She didn't get far. Before she'd taken more than a step or two into the empty space, she stopped and doubled over in pain. A feeling of dread filled her stomach and she knew beyond a shadow of a doubt that the west wing was a bad place. Although Anie couldn't take another step forward, her sister wasn't afflicted by whatever premonition had rooted Anie to the floor. The younger girl walked quickly past.

"STOP!" Anie yelled as loud as she could.

Normally if she'd yelled at her sibling like that their mother would have been angry and would have insisted on an explanation and an apology, but not that day. Instead, their mother only agreed that they shouldn't walk any farther into the west wing and didn't question Anie at all. It was as if she'd picked up on something too.

Later that week the family went on a ghost tour of the city. When they passed the museum, the tour guide, with a dark hood framing her head and an old-fashioned lantern held aloft, paused and told the assembled tourists and thrill-seekers about the building's fourth floor — specifically, the west wing.

Countless people, both museum staff and visitors, have seen doors swing open and shut on their own. People often feel like they're being watched when they're all alone. The elevators travel up and down despite being empty. Unnatural cold and hot spots materialize with no explanation. Alarms go off for no reason. Vacuum cords have been yanked out of electrical outlets while janitors try to clean the floors. Security guards have been grabbed by invisible hands; many have sacrificed a day of pay when assigned the graveyard shift on the fourth floor, and a guard quit after one night spent in the old, spooky museum.

The building's official name is the Victoria Memorial Museum Building.

A woman called Mary, who worked at the museum for many years, was skeptical of the ghost stories. But one morning, while she was walking through the fourth floor, her opinion suddenly changed. It was 9:55 a.m. and the museum would open in five minutes, but at that moment Mary was all alone. Or so she thought. Suddenly she was overcome by the sensation that there was someone creeping up behind her, and that the spirit — yes, she was already starting to believe in ghosts — desired nothing more than to scare her.

"It's okay," Mary said to herself in an attempt to calm her nerves. "The museum is not really haunted." But the belief that not only was the museum haunted, but the ghost was right behind her took hold as her heart began to pump faster and her palms grew sweaty. Mary stopped in front of a mirror and looked at her reflection, standing alone in the large, empty room. But then, just before she turned to leave, a cloud of grey fog appeared behind her. It swirled in the air, and the head, shoulders and arms of a tall man appeared within it.

Mary's body grew so cold that she felt like she'd been dunked in ice water. The ghost approached her silently. Although her mind was screaming at her body to go, flee, *run!*, she couldn't move a muscle. The man then walked straight through her, and she felt incredibly hot — as if a great surge of electricity had run through her veins. Mary watched as the man carried on for a few more steps . . . and then disappeared.

The most unusual sighting of all took place in the Fossil Gallery. Amidst the reconstructed skeletons and life-sized models of dinosaurs, Mary has seen a dark shadow travel across the floor in what she describes as a "wave-like motion." Had she found the courage to peel her eyes off the floor and look up, would she have seen the ghost of a prehistoric flying creatures, such as a pterodactyl or pteranodon, flying overhead?

There are many theories as to who the ghost (the *human* ghost) is. Some believe it's David Ewart, the architect who designed the building and oversaw its construction between 1905 and 1910. The museum was constructed on unstable clay, causing the building to sink, heave and crack in many places. In 1915 three storeys of the tower were removed to remedy the problem, and some believe Ewart was so upset by this change that he returned after his death. Others believe the ghost might be Sir Wilfrid Laurier, seventh prime minister of Canada, since his body lay in state in the museum for three days after he died in 1919. Some staff members think it might be the ghost of one of the ancient Egyptian mummies that used to be stored in the basement. And an exorcist who was called in by the museum in 1989 claims to have made contact with the spirit of a Cree man from British Columbia, whose clothing was part of a display at the time.

With so many different theories, it's hard to pinpoint the source of the ghostly activity in the museum. Of course, it's always possible there is more than one spirit in the building, so when you visit the Canadian Museum of Nature, make sure to look up when passing through the Fossil Gallery, and behind you when passing through the fourth floor.

BEAR ATTACK

Connoire Bay, Newfoundland and Labrador

It was a cool, crisp fall night in the late 1960s when James, a man from the town of Burgeo, was drifting off to sleep. He was settled in a small cabin he had recently purchased in the woods near Connoire Bay. The cabin had been sold many times over the years — it was as if no one was able or willing to stay there for long. And when James had seen that it was up for sale, he decided to purchase it for himself, despite any misgivings or unease he might have felt.

The night was dark, the forest chilly and peaceful. James's eyelids began to close and his mind slipped toward dreams, but he was shocked wide awake by a jarring sound. He sat bolt upright in bed and listened.

Scratch-scratch-scritch.

It sounded like a bear clawing at the side of the cabin . . . looking for a way inside.

James leapt out of his bed and loaded his gun, then took up a position in front of the door and aimed the barrel at it. He waited. The scratching continued, and James followed the source of the sound. It passed by the front door but the bear didn't break through. Instead, it continued to circle the cabin, scratching at the walls. This lasted all night, preventing James from getting any sleep. He peered out the windows but could see only darkness. He only had an old oil lamp. Without a flashlight he couldn't see the creature with his own eyes, and he had no desire to venture out into the dark. But when the sun finally rose in the early morning, the scratching suddenly vanished.

An extensive search of the area and the cabin's exterior walls revealed no sign or trace that anything had tried to claw its way in throughout the night, but that gave James little comfort. He was exhausted, so he slept through the day. But before night fell, he placed fresh mud on the ground all around the cabin, like a moat, in the hopes that — if the nighttime creature should return — its paw prints would be captured for examination the following day. With his plan in place and the moon rising in the sky, James went to bed.

Scratch-scratch-scritch! Scratch-scratch-scritch! Scratch-scratch-scritch!

The bear was back, but now it sounded like it had doubled its efforts to get in. And not only that, but it was on the roof right above his head, ferociously attacking the shingles. As he had the night before, James got out of bed and loaded his gun, then stayed awake all night in case the bear — he was more certain than ever it was a bear, but he had no idea how it had gotten up on the roof — managed to break in. Fortunately it didn't, although it did scratch and claw at the roof all night. When the sun rose, the commotion ended.

At least the bear would have left its tracks in the mud around the cabin, and then James would be able to see how big it was and maybe get a hint about how it managed to get up on the roof. But when he searched the cabin's perimeter, he couldn't find a single track. That was impossible. He had spent two nights awake with fright as he listened to the bear try to claw its way in. How it hadn't left a single paw print, James couldn't fathom.

He had one last desperate idea to afford himself a little extra protection for the night ahead. He nailed a small piece of wood to the door, which prevented it from closing all the way while maintaining a barrier between him and the beast. His plan was to stay up one more time with his gun already loaded and pointed through the small opening. As soon as the bear passed by, James would shoot it without hesitation. If it returned — and James had no reason to believe it wouldn't — he'd be ready for it. He took up his post inside the cabin.

The sun set. Night fell. The woods grew quiet and still, but only for a moment.

The bear began its attack on the cabin immediately, and from the sound of the scratching on the wooden boards it was angrier and more vicious than ever. The walls shook and the sounds were both deafening and terrifying.

SCRATCH-SCRATCH-SCRITCH! SCRATCH-SCRATCH-SCRITCH! SCRATCH-SCRATCH-SCRITCH!

James swallowed dryly and readied to squeeze the trigger. He listened as the bear clawed at the cabin and moved closer to the door, closer, closer . . .

But then, just when the bear should have appeared through the opening, the sound passed by the open door and continued on the other side of it. James hadn't seen anything pass, because nothing *had* passed. At least, nothing he could see. But he *had* heard it, and that was perhaps worse than if it had appeared in the flesh before him.

For the third night in a row, the ceaseless assault lasted until the sun rose. At that time, James immediately packed up and fled from the cabin. He was exhausted, fed up and frightened, and he wasn't willing to spend one more night there. He was so upset that he couldn't bring himself to tell anyone about the experience for a number of years, not even his wife and children. Perhaps talking about the ordeal was too scary, like reliving it all over again. He certainly could never return, especially not with his family, so he sold the cabin to someone else. The new buyer didn't own the cabin long before he too had to get rid of it. And the next buyer quickly decided to move the cabin farther inland, as if it was the location on Connoire Bay that was cursed or haunted, not the cabin itself.

And maybe that was true. Just a few days after the cabin was moved, a horrible storm ravaged the area where it had once stood. Giant waves crashed on the shore and pushed large rocks, some weighing nearly twenty-five kilograms each, great distances across the land. Once the storm died down, it was discovered that the spot where the cabin had stood was covered by rocks and gravel. The cabin, had it been there, would have been crushed . . . along with anyone who might have been inside.

PHANTOM FLIGHT

Airdrie, Alberta

Little did Clive know when he picked up his ringing phone one day in February 1992 that he was about to take the strangest call of his entire life.

On the other end of the line was a worker from the Airdrie Airport, a short drive northeast from Clive's home in Calgary. Clive owned a small plane, a 1940s Piper J-3 Cub, that he had restored at the airport. But the plane wasn't acting as any plane should. In fact, it was acting as if it was possessed.

The airport worker told Clive that strange things had happened. Clive's plane had been securely fastened, with each wing and the tail tied down, but it had somehow broken free of its bonds, taken off, flown a short distance away and landed right on top of another small plane, where it had finally come to a rest. And it had done all this without a pilot.

Clive hung up the phone, took a moment to process what he'd been told, then grabbed his wife and rushed north to Airdrie. There were three witnesses to the bizarre event and all of them were either aircraft owners or airport mechanics with no reason to lie, so Clive couldn't find any way to discredit the story. Furthermore, all three of the witnesses were shaken by what they'd seen and clearly a little apprehensive to approach the possessed plane. When they led Clive to it, he found his plane exactly as they'd said: on top of another aircraft.

But it hadn't landed *exactly* as Clive had expected. It was upside down. The fact that his plane was balanced on top of another without falling off seemed to defy the laws of gravity. Its tail rudder was impossibly balanced on the other craft's rudder, both of which were rounded and only twelve millimetres wide. If his plane had been positioned a millimetre or two to either side, it would have slipped and crashed to the ground. To make this landing would have been impossible for a human, but apparently not for whatever spirit had flown it earlier that day.

A gust of wind kicked up and blew Clive's plane's rudder off of the other plane's rudder. Clive's plane fell with a loud *clunk* that made everyone jump. His plane was still atop the other, but at least Clive could now tie them both in place so no more damage would occur if the wind got any worse. He'd deal with righting the plane the following morning.

But before anyone could leave in search of rope, the

A 1940s Piper J-3 Cub

J-3 Cub lifted straight up off the other plane and into the air. Everyone jumped back in fright. Empty, the plane flew away from the shocked spectators, heading south and still upside down. It accelerated rapidly and pulled into an incredibly steep climb. One of the pilots told the others that there was no possible way that type of plane could pull off such a manoeuvre — they simply weren't built to do so.

Once it was about 100 metres up in the sky, it did a loop in the air and flew straight back down to the runway, where it made a perfect three-point landing and taxied back to the other plane, stopping less than a metre away from it. Clive and the others stood in silence with their mouths hanging wide open. They were all in complete shock.

In retrospect, Clive realized he'd had an eerie feeling about the plane almost as soon as he'd purchased it. He'd gotten it at a great price because it needed some work, and at first he was a little hesitant because he knew it might be difficult to find parts and make repairs to a fifty-year-old plane. But the entire process had gone incredibly smoothly — perhaps too smoothly. It was as if fate was on Clive's side and there was an extra, unseen set of hands helping him along the way.

After watching the J-3 Cub fly on its own and make an incredible landing, Clive decided to do a little research into it. He discovered that the plane's previous owner was a pilot who had died a short while before, when the helicopter he was flying crashed in the Yukon. The deceased pilot's family contracted an auction company to quickly sell off his private collection of aircraft, and that's how Clive had gotten such a good deal on the J-3 Cub. But had he known that the plane he'd just taken possession of was itself possessed by the ghost of a pilot who refused to leave the cockpit, Clive might not have seen the deal as being half as good as he'd thought.

THE HEADLESS GHOST

Woodridge, Manitoba

Tucked away in the woods, one hour southeast of Winnipeg, is the town of Woodridge. People visit to cottage and camp, enjoying the isolation and natural beauty of the area. A crisscrossing network of blueberry trails snakes through the surrounding forests, perfect for all-terrain vehicles in the summer and snowmobiles in the winter. The town was established when the Canadian National Railway (CN) built tracks through the area in the early 1900s, and a ghost was created when one of the townsfolk lost his head on the tracks in the 1920s.

A CN maintenance worker and his family were the first people to make the ghost's grim acquaintance. They lived in a company-supplied house near the tracks just out-side town, beside an old, abandoned church and a small, neglected cemetery. Late at night, after the worker and his family had gone upstairs to sleep, they always heard the dull *clomp-clomp-clomp* of a man's feet walking to and fro on the main floor. Over time the nighttime noises grew louder and more unnerving, as the ghost began making a racket, hammering boards and rattling chains. This happened every single night, but the source of the sounds was never spotted.

The worker's son was the first member of the family to see anything unusual. He caught sight of one of his marbles shaking in its jar as if from a light tremor in the ground. And then, without warning, the marble flew out of the jar and across the room; the boy felt like his heart might follow suit and fly out of his mouth to land beside the marble that was skittering across the floor. Before he could scream or run out of the room, however, the rest of his marbles soared out of the jar, crashed on the floor, and streaked in countless different directions.

On a cold winter night, the boy's mother was outside taking their clothes off the line when she looked up and saw a man walk past silently. He held an old-fashioned oil lantern in front of his face as he trudged toward the remains of the nearby church, then entered it. He did not pause to greet the woman. He did not even seem to be aware of her presence, which made her feel uncomfortable and distressed. She ran inside and told her husband about the stranger. He immediately raced to the church to investigate but found it to be empty. Not only that, but other than his own tracks, there weren't any footprints in the snow anywhere around the old building — heading neither into it nor out.

Over the years many hunters and outdoor enthusiasts have looked behind them to see the ghost following their path. Dogs bred to hunt have run away to hide, and the canines can hardly be blamed. When the ghost raises his lantern, the light sometimes reveals a full man, but other times it reveals two legs, two arms and a torso . . . but no head.

When asked who the ghost might be and how he lost his head, locals tell variations of the same story. The most commonly accepted one is that he was a well-known Woodridge man named Joe, who lived alone in the woods and made a weekly pilgrimage into town to meet his friends at the local pub. One night in the pub, tall tales were told, songs were sung, drinks were drunk and time passed quickly. Old Joe lit his kerosene lamp and hobbled back into the night, stumbling along the tracks to his house.

The next morning, the townsfolk made a gruesome discovery. Joe's body was lying beside the train tracks, but his head was not. It was widely accepted that he had fallen on the tracks as a train passed, severing his head clean off his shoulders. Joe's head was never discovered, likely dragged off into the bush by a wild animal.

An interesting thing has happened to Joe's ghost since the mid-1900s. He's still seen in the woods surrounding Woodridge, particularly near the train tracks. But he no longer appears in human form. Instead people spot a glowing orb that hovers two metres off the forest floor and glides effortlessly through trees, sometimes accompanied by unearthly groans and moans. The light has been known to change colour, size and brightness — one woman said it was bright enough to blind her if she had mistakenly looked directly at it.

Journalist Jasmine Van Gerwen recalls her grandfather's account of spotting the ghostly light as it approached him near the outskirts of town. It stopped when it was less than two metres away before continuing on its way and disappearing in the distance.

In 1975 local resident Gary Auch was parked in the area when he happened to look in his rear-view mirror and spot the light moving up and down above his trunk.

The most commonly held belief is that the light is Joe's kerosene lamp, as if his body has faded away but the light source he carried on the night he met a most unfortunate fate can never be snuffed out. However, there is another theory, and it's much grislier. A small group of locals, including Van Gerwen's grandfather, believe the orb is Joe's decapitated head, doomed to an eternity of floating through the woods, always in search of the body that was removed from the scene of his death nearly a century ago.

CHILD'S PLAY

Regina, Saskatchewan

Lowell's legs were falling asleep and his back ached. He was hiding in the bottom of a dusty cupboard that had sat unused in a corner of the farmhouse's basement for a long time. It was pitch-black in the cupboard and as hot as an oven. Sweat ran down his body in thick rivulets. A spider crawled up his bare leg, but Lowell ignored it, refusing to move a muscle or make a sound. He couldn't hear what was happening on the other side of the cupboard doors.

By now his brother and sister were probably growing frustrated at not being able to find Lowell. They were playing hide-and-seek during a summer vacation spent at their grandparents' farmhouse, and nine-year-old Lowell was just small enough to squeeze into the cupboard. He'd been waiting silently for a very long time. And although he couldn't see or hear his siblings, he assumed they'd probably given up looking for him by now.

Lowell pushed on the doors. They didn't budge. He pushed a little harder. They still didn't open. He rammed his shoulder against the wood, but nothing happened. That's when he started to panic. He kicked and pounded and yelled and screamed as loud as he could manage.

But then he heard something that made him quiet down in a hurry. It was a man's voice, and he sounded so close that it seemed like he was speaking directly inside Lowell's head.

"You're trapped," the unseen man said in a tone that was laced with malice. "Let's see how you like hiding now."

Terror consumed Lowell. Not only did he resume screaming and pounding against the doors with his hands and feet, he started ramming his head against the wood in a mad attempt to escape. Suddenly the doors opened and he tumbled out of the cupboard and into the cool air of the basement. He landed on the dirty floor at his siblings' feet. They both looked down at Lowell in confusion.

His sister asked how he had gotten himself into the cupboard. After Lowell explained that he had squeezed inside, contorted his body to fit and then closed the doors with his fingernails, his sister shook her head. She wasn't surprised that he had been able to fit inside the cupboard; she was in shock that he had somehow managed to push a heavy trunk in front of the cupboard doors, barricading himself in. That's why his siblings hadn't bothered to look inside the cupboard — they didn't see any way he could be in there.

Lowell saw the trail in the dirt from the cupboard to the wall where the trunk had been moved by his siblings, but who had put it in front of the cupboard in the first place? The three children raced out of the basement and never played down there again, not even when the weather prevented them from playing outside.

Lowell never told anyone other than his sister and brother about what had happened. By the time summer ended and the three children returned home, the event had largely been forgotten. But twenty years later, Lowell and his father were having a conversation when he mentioned that he and his siblings hadn't enjoyed staying with their grandparents. Both of his grandparents were strict disciplinarians and his grandfather, Lowell admitted, punished them for small things and accused them of being disrespectful and lazy.

Lowell's father agreed that his father could be tough, but he revealed that his own grandfather — Lowell's great-grandfather — was *really* mean. To illustrate this point, Lowell's father told his son a story. It was eerily familiar.

One day when he was a young boy, Lowell's father hadn't done his chores and Lowell's great-grandfather was irate. Fearing for his safety, the boy ran downstairs to find a place to hide. He came across the cupboard in the corner of the basement. He bent his head, crammed his body into the cupboard and closed the door behind him, but it was too late. His grandfather had followed him and knew exactly where he was hiding. The boy heard the sound of something heavy being dragged across the floor and slammed against the cupboard's doors.

"Let's see how you like hiding now," the old man barked from the other side of the doors. He left his grandson trapped in the cupboard for an hour before finally releasing the hot, sore and frightened boy.

When his father had finished telling this disturbing tale, Lowell kept his own similar story to himself — his father clearly didn't want to discuss it any further and promptly changed the subject. But Lowell finally knew who had trapped him in the cupboard twenty years before. And he realized he was lucky his siblings were there to let him out. If not, who knows how long Lowell would have been trapped in the cupboard by the ghost of his great-grandfather, a man who clearly had no patience for child's play.

THE DEATH MASK

Woodstock, Ontario

Convicted criminal Isaiah Wright was not the type of man to frighten easily, but one night in 1903 he had more than enough reason to nearly lose his mind with fright. Wright was a prisoner in the Oxford County Jail, an old building he knew all too well. He made a habit of getting himself arrested and pleading guilty to petty crimes in order to be housed in the jail throughout the long winter months. He deeply regretted this habit the night he saw a ghost float past his cell — number thirteen — three times. It was after the third appearance of the ghost that Wright began to scream at the top of his lungs and was found in a corner of his cell huddled in a tight ball, shaking uncontrollably and muttering incomprehensibly.

Wright wasn't the only prisoner to see the ghost that

year — many other inmates also reported seeing the ghost fly past their cells. When he was released, he informed Governor Cameron that he would not be committing any more petty crimes, nor would he be returning the following winter. Seeing a ghost in the jail had scared him out of a life of crime.

There are a few theories about the ghost that haunts the old jail, which is now the Oxford County Board of Health building, but the most prevalent belief is that it is Thomas Cook. Large and quick-tempered, Cook had a terrible reputation in the town as a fighter and alcoholic and was generally feared by all. In 1862 he was convicted of killing his second wife and was ordered to be executed on December 16 of that year. He was to be hanged in the jail courtyard, and more than three thousand citizens attended to watch. They didn't know it yet, but what they were about to witness would be far more gruesome than anything they ever could have imagined.

Cook was led to the gallows at 10:55 a.m. The executioner was a man from the community, but his identity was concealed by an odd disguise that consisted of a white towel pulled across his mouth and nose, a pair of goggles over his eyes and an old white hat on top of his head. Cook broke out in prayer as the rope was slipped over his head and tightened around his neck. The lever was pulled at 11 a.m. Cook passed through the trap door, but he was so heavy that his head was completely severed from his body when the rope snapped taut. His lifeless trunk fell to the ground and his head rolled a metre away in the dirt before coming to a stop. The crowd was stunned into silence for a long time. Cook was so loathed that some spectators were disappointed they hadn't been able to see him swing by his neck.

Following a macabre custom of the day, a death mask of Cook's face was made and placed near the entrance to the jail. The death mask is still there today, staring out with dead-looking eyes, downturned lips and a cracked nose.

Cook's body was given to his friends for burial, but someone from the Woodstock Medical Clinic purchased the remains for medical research. It is unlikely Cook would have ever consented to this, but of course he didn't have the opportunity to object. He did not receive a proper burial.

In 1903, around the time the ghost of the Oxford County Jail first appeared and terrorized inmate Isaiah Wright, a work crew unearthed human remains at Finkle and Dundas Streets, where the Woodstock Medical Centre was once situated. The bones were identified as belonging to Cook.

The ghost continued to haunt the building, and a renovation project in the 1980s seemingly increased the level of paranormal activity. Ernie Hunt was in charge of the project and noticed right away that there was something very unusual in the courthouse. When he was updating the plumbing, he'd lay out all of his materials on a scaffold on the third floor before leaving for the day so that everything was ready for him the next morning . . . only that never panned out the way he hoped. When he'd arrive at work, he'd find all of those items in the boiler room on the main

Thomas Cook's death mask at the Oxford County Jail

floor. No one had been in the building through the night.

Hunt and his team converted an old chimney into an elevator shaft. Hunt decided to leave his tools and materials in the elevator at night since he could lock it up and ensure that no one could move his things. But sure enough, although everything was completely inaccessible and no one else had been in the building, he'd find missing items in the boiler room each day.

The elevator was operated by a key, but that didn't stop the ghost from using it to travel from floor to floor. One Sunday, Hunt and the county engineer were working late when the elevator suddenly started up all by itself, despite the fact that the necessary key was in Hunt's pocket. As Hunt and the engineer watched in amazement — and a little fear — the elevator's lights indicated that it opened on the fourth floor, then the third and then the second. Finally, it reached the main floor and the doors opened, but no one was inside. Hunt tried to laugh it off by joking that he hadn't seen anyone exit the elevator. But the next day he called the technician, who informed him that what he claimed had happened was impossible — the elevator would not, under normal circumstances, open on a floor without the use of the key. But Hunt was quickly coming to realize that these weren't normal circumstances.

A little while later the elevator drama took a much scarier turn. Hunt's wife and their eighteen-month-old grandson were visiting him at work when the elevator once again turned itself on and the doors opened wide. The young boy ran onto the elevator before either of his grandparents could stop him. The doors closed, trapping him inside alone. The elevator travelled up to the fourth floor, then down to the third, then back to the fourth. Hunt and his wife were on the main floor, but they could hear their grandson screaming in terror the entire time. They raced up the stairs to the third floor and managed to open the door when the elevator returned there, then frantically grabbed the terrified boy.

Hunt was regularly overwhelmed by the feeling of being watched, and he'd often see a passing shadow out of the corner of his eye. Time and again someone would tap his shoulder from behind, but when Hunt turned around he would find that he was completely alone. And then one day when he was in the tunnels beneath the building with a couple of other workers, he finally caught sight of what he believed to be Cook's ghost. They turned a dark corner and came face to face with the misty form of Cook's head and shoulders, a frightening sight that disappeared before their eyes.

Thanks to the death mask of Thomas Cook that still hangs on the outside of the building, anyone who visits the old courthouse can confront the convicted criminal turned ghost without needing to enter the tunnels. But if you need to reach an upper floor, taking the stairs would be best.

VOICES IN THE VAULTS

St. John's, Newfoundland and Labrador

Some time in the late 1800s, after a long, gruelling day of work, two men — both employees of Newman & Company, an import-export trade company that had been shipping goods since the early 1500s — decided to help themselves to a glass of Newman's famed port wine. This was strictly forbidden — employees were not allowed to drink the product — but the men ensured that they were alone in the stone vaults on Water Street and then perused their options. They found an old unmarked barrel and figured that no one would notice if they took one glass from it. After a final glance at their surroundings, they set to work prying the barrel open.

The moment they popped the lid off, an unearthly moan echoed throughout the tunnel. The men froze. After a moment they realized they were still alone and dismissed the sound as nothing but the wind and their nerves getting the best of them.

One of the men dunked a glass into the barrel, took a sip of port and then passed the glass to his friend. As he enjoyed a drink, the moaning began again, louder than before. Perhaps they weren't alone after all. Fearing that someone might catch them in the act, they decided to investigate the vaults, but after a thorough search they were certain there was no one else inside with them. They once again shrugged off the odd sounds they'd heard and returned to the open barrel, then continued to drink.

One glass became two, then three, four and five. As he went to fill the cup for the sixth time, something unusual caught the man's eye. There seemed to be something submerged in the barrel. He handed the cup to his friend and shook the barrel in an attempt to see what was hidden at the bottom. Moaning filled the vaults, this time so loud that there could be no mistake: the sound was not being caused by the wind.

As panic started to seize both men, the first reached his hands deep into the port, desperate to find what was hidden there and somehow convinced that there was a connection between it and the moaning. His submerged hands touched something a little larger than a bowling ball and he grabbed what felt like short, curly bits of string. He pulled the mystery object out of the barrel and was horrified to discover he was holding a human head.

He dropped the head back into the barrel with a splash and staggered backwards as the second man spat out a

The vaults of Newman & Company

mouthful of the tainted port. Apparently, another Newman & Company employee had died aboard a ship that was sailing from England to Newfoundland, and his head had been preserved in an unmarked barrel of port for the journey home. To say that the two men picked the wrong barrel to steal from would be a gross understatement.

Although the two men who discovered the head in the barrel heard a ghost but didn't see it, another employee encountered a spirit in the flesh, so to speak, only a few years later. He entered a little-used area of the vaults and came face to face with the terrifying vision of a woman standing with her back to the opposite wall. She stared at him with a mournful expression, then raised her arms and slowly approached. Her hands were shackled but she didn't make a sound.

The employee ran away and told Mr. Newman, his employer, what he had seen. The two men returned to the room. They didn't find the ghost, but they did make an unusual discovery. In an old, musty barrel surrounded by cargo from a past freighter run, they found a wooden box covered with intricate carvings. Something inside rattled when Newman shook it gently. He opened the lid and found that it was full of bones. Human bones. Also in the barrel was a bundle of blood-red silk and a pair of iron shackles. Beneath the silk was a human skull. Fearful that leaving the bones untouched would prevent the ghost from moving on, Newman decided to gather the remains in order to give the woman — whoever she had been — a proper burial.

It worked. The ghost of the woman was never seen in the vaults again, but she did appear a short while later in one of Newman's dreams. She beckoned him to approach and warned him that a great tragedy was to befall one of his ships. When Newman awoke early the next morning and recalled the dream, he began to panic. He hadn't insured that particular ship and he'd be bankrupt if anything happened to it, so he decided not to tempt fate and immediately had it insured.

The ship never reached its destination in England and was believed to have sunk somewhere along the way. Is it possible that the ghost appeared in Newman's dream to save his business in thanks for the proper burial he gave her remains?

Although that ghost was never seen again, other spirits continue to make their presence known to this day. Kelli-ann Blackwood worked in the Newman Wine Vaults in 2003 and 2004, and often felt as if she'd walked through cold spots that enveloped her in an emotionally distraught feeling that would remain with her for the rest of the day. Other days she and her fellow employees would hear phantom footsteps that seemed to be coming from within the stone walls. Invisible hands would brush up against their arms as they passed the barrels, and the spirits sometimes pinched the living, as if out of malice. Some heard voices calling their names when no one else was in the building.

On June 18, 2011, Karen Hanlon caught one of the Newman Wine Vaults' ghosts on camera. She was attending a small private wedding in the building when she took a picture of a couple of musicians playing at one end of a tunnel. Hovering in the air above a mixing board was the foggy yet remarkably clear image of a man in a white dress shirt, his face dark and obscured. Karen took one look at her camera's digital screen and raced to find the newlywed couple.

"Look what I just took!" she shouted, waving the camera in the air. "Look what I just took! There's somebody in the picture."

The question is, which ghost did Karen catch? In the Newman Wine Vaults, it could've been one of many. There's no shortage of spirits floating among the wine.

THE SCREAMING DOPPELGÄNGER

Victoria, British Columbia

Beacon Hill Park in downtown Victoria is one of the most well-loved and beautiful locations in the city. The 200 acres of land was officially established as a park in 1882 and contains walking paths, landscaped grounds, bridges, ponds and rivers, and many breeds of trees, flowers and animals. But it's also home to a ghost. What follows has been described as one of the strangest paranormal events ever documented anywhere in the world.

Victoria resident Peter Stewart and his wife loved Beacon Hill Park. They enjoyed waking before the sun and going for long jogs along the park's many paths before other people started to arrive. Their regular route took them past a rocky area near the corner of Douglas and Superior Streets and they rarely saw another soul there so early in the morning — but that changed in the early 1980s.

One day they turned a corner at a decent pace and stopped dead in their tracks. A most unusual sight met their eyes. A woman was standing atop the rocks. At first they thought she was holding a yoga position, but when they took a closer look they realized this was not the case. Her legs were spread shoulder-width apart and her arms were stretched up to the sky. She was facing east, toward the rising sun. The woman was slim and tanned, had blond hair and wore a black shirt and white pants. The odd thing about her was that her head was tilted back and her mouth was open in a silent scream. She looked like she was in terrible pain, but she stood statue-still with her eyes closed. She didn't acknowledge Peter and his wife at all, so eventually the joggers moved on.

They saw the silently screaming woman many times, and so did others. She always matched the same description, was only seen on the rocks as the sun rose, and never moved nor made a sound. One woman out walking her dog asked her if she needed any help, but even that didn't elicit a reaction. Two groundskeepers responsible for cleaning the park early in the morning saw her regularly, and they thought it was odd that they never once saw her enter or leave.

On November 15, 1983, the groundskeepers made a gruesome discovery. It was a beautiful fall day and the ground was covered in bright red, orange and yellow leaves. But they found an odd pile of leaves, all bunched up behind the rocks where the silent woman had always been seen. Sticking out from that pile was the toe of a woman's shoe. The men called the park authorities. When the police arrived soon after, the two groundskeepers were asked to stay nearby so that they could answer any questions the officers might have. And so they were there when the police removed the body.

The groundskeepers couldn't believe their eyes. It was the same woman, the one who stood on the rocks most mornings. But the woman looked a little different. Instead of tanned skin and blond hair, she had pale skin and black hair. Instead of a black shirt and white pants, she wore a white shirt and black pants. It was as if the woman seen on the rocks was a photo negative version of the body found in the same area, with the colour of her skin, hair and clothes reversed.

There's a German word for this: doppelgänger, or a "double walker." A doppelgänger is the ghost of a person who is still alive. Everyone who had seen the woman on the rocks — who came to be known as the Screaming Doppelgänger — knew at once that she was the ghost of the murdered woman.

An autopsy was performed on the body and revealed that she had been strangled before being left in the park. Her husband had reported her missing several weeks earlier.

What's particularly interesting and eerie about this case is that the woman's doppelgänger was seen for years before she was murdered, and that she looked like a photo negative version of herself. But that was about to change.

Six weeks after reading about the murder in the

newspaper, Peter and his wife were jogging through the park when they saw the ghost of the woman again. She was standing in the exact same spot on the rocks, with her feet shoulder-width apart, her arms stretched up to the sky, facing the rising sun. Her head was back and her mouth was open wide in a silent scream. But now the ghost looked exactly like the body that had been removed from the park, with pale skin and black hair.

The stunned couple stopped and stared at the ghost for a short while before she disappeared in front of their eyes.

The Screaming Doppelgänger is still seen today, but with every passing year her body grows more vaporous and misty, and less corporeal. Since her murder remains unsolved, there's no telling how long she'll continue to terrify early risers in Beacon Hill Park.

THE SHADOWY FIGURE

Duncan, British Columbia

It started with a chill that was far too cold to be normal, and before long Marianne Sisler knew that she was being haunted by a ghost.

Marianne and a co-worker were the only two people in the office one Friday afternoon in 1975. Marianne was in the front reception area when she decided she needed a coffee to see her through the rest of the day. She was tired and under a lot of stress. Her husband had suffered a stroke a few months before and spent most of his time in bed, unable to move very well. And her mother, a widow, was beginning to need more attention and care.

Marianne made her way to the lunchroom at the back of the office and poured herself a cup of coffee. As she walked back to reception, a terrible feeling suddenly stopped her.

She felt impossibly cold air swirling around her legs. It felt more like a presence than a draft.

Marianne stepped to the side and realized she'd been standing in a cold spot. She stepped back in the spot, but the odd sensation had vanished.

She looked around and saw that her co-worker was at her desk with her head down. Marianne was relieved she wouldn't have to explain why she'd stopped in the hall and stepped from side to side. She felt a little silly. After all, it had only been a bit of cold. More than likely there was a perfectly reasonable explanation.

By the time Marianne got home she had forgotten all about the incident. After dinner she got busy in the kitchen preparing food for the weekend. Her husband was in bed and the house was otherwise empty. She was at the counter with her back to the rest of the room when suddenly the hair on the back of her neck stood on end. She knew someone was behind her, staring at her. Her husband? Impossible. Marianne would have heard him approach. An intruder? Unlikely. She knew for a fact that she had locked both the front and back doors.

With a sense of apprehension, Marianne slowly turned around to find a shadowy figure passing through the kitchen and into the living room, out of view. She could see that it wore a men's dark grey suit, but the man's face and hands were obscured as if they were made of shadows. Even so, Marianne felt certain that the shadow man was her father, who had died more than twenty years earlier.

She couldn't move for a moment. Then, once her nerves began to settle, she didn't know what to do other than continue with her work. But only a few minutes later Marianne felt the same sensation on the back of her neck. She turned and saw the shadow pass through the kitchen and into the living room once more. This time he disappeared into thin air.

Marianne quickly finished her work and retreated to her bedroom. Her husband was already in a deep sleep. She got into bed and pulled the covers up over her face, leaving only the top of her head exposed.

Before long, she felt something touching her hair. It was a gentle touch, light as a feather, but still unnerving. She pulled the covers down just enough to peek out. The shadow man was standing beside her bed. Quickly she pulled the covers back over her head, hiding from view completely.

The next morning Marianne reflected on the previous day's events. She didn't share the details with anyone and slowly began to convince herself that all of it — the cold spot, the shadowy ghost, the feeling of her hair being touched — had been her imagination. It was far easier to believe that the feelings and visions had been stress induced. Surely she'd feel a little better after a good night's sleep.

Marianne's grown daughter, Sandra, soon arrived. They had arranged to go shopping together. They chatted about work in the kitchen for a while, but Marianne didn't mention the previous day.

After a while Sandra went upstairs to freshen up before going out. When she returned, she had a very unusual question for her mother: "Do you believe in ghosts?"

The question took Marianne by surprise, so she asked her daughter why she wanted to know.

Sandra was unwilling to explain.

"Did you see him?" Marianne asked.

Sandra admitted that she had seen the reflection of a shadowy man pass behind her while she was brushing her hair.

"You saw your grandfather," Marianne said.

Marianne's father remained in the house for the rest of the week, moving silently from room to room, causing chills to spread across Marianne's body every time he was near. Sandra visited twice that week. Both times she declared, "He is still here, Mom!"

The following Saturday, eight days after Marianne had first felt her father's cold presence, Marianne woke up and immediately knew that he had moved on.

Sandra returned later that day and agreed. "Oh, he is gone now," she said as soon as she entered the house.

On Sunday Marianne visited her mother. Before much time had passed, and without comment, her mother handed her a photograph. Marianne looked at it in surprise. It was an old black-and-white photo of her father that she had never seen before. In it he was wearing the exact same dark grey suit he had worn throughout the week.

Marianne felt like her mother must have given her that particular picture at that moment for a reason, so she told her mother what both she and Sandra had seen in her home.

Her mother listened silently. When Marianne was finished, her mother made no comment. Marianne wondered if she had also seen the shadow in the suit or if the timing of her sharing the photograph had been a coincidence.

She never discovered the truth.

Marianne's mother passed away in October of 1979. The evening of the funeral, Marianne was alone in her den when the telephone rang loudly, interrupting the silence of the darkened house. She answered the phone.

"Hello?" she said.

No one responded. The connection was bad, as though someone were calling long-distance.

"Hello?" she said again.

"Lottie! Lottie!" a voice screamed in her ear.

Marianne recognized the voice immediately. It was her mother.

"Mom, this is Marianne!"

Silence. Although the line remained open for several minutes and Marianne waited, listening intently, her mother said nothing else. Eventually Marianne hung up. When she picked up the receiver again, the line was clear.

Marianne couldn't believe what had happened. Lottie was her mother's best friend, and both women had lived in the same seniors' residence.

To have one parent try to make contact after death was shocking enough, but to have both do so was nearly unfathomable. What Marianne's parents had hoped to achieve are mysteries that will remain unsolved forever.

DEATH IN THE DINING ROOM

Halifax, Nova Scotia

Lunch was over, dinner was yet to come, and the dining room was empty. A waitress at the Halifax Club took the opportunity to get caught up on tasks that had to be completed before the next rush — the members-only meeting place was often quite busy at meal times. She bustled around the room, clearing dirty dishes and taking them to the kitchen, placing clean tablecloths on each of the tables, rolling napkins and setting clean cutlery and glasses. There was plenty to do, but her work was going well and she felt good about the progress she was making. But then there was a disturbance in the dining room that made her pause.

She heard the high-pitched sound of glass hitting glass. Not shattering, but clinking loudly. She dropped the cutlery she'd been about to set and stood straight up, whipping her head left and right, scanning the room. She was alone.

Straining her ears, she listened. There it was again, glass on glass. She checked each one of the dining room's tables but there was nothing she could find that was making the sound. And yet it persisted.

Finally, after her nerves had stretched as tight as they possibly could, the waitress looked up. The chandeliers were all swinging violently from side to side. That was impossible — the doors and windows were all closed — but they were swinging all the same. The only explanation the woman could think of for the swinging chandeliers was that the Halifax Club's former general manager was in the room with her.

He often is. In fact, he never leaves. Not even death can keep him away from his workplace. His spirit can't be blamed for lingering. His death — right there in the dining room where many odd things happen — was both shocking and gruesome.

The Halifax Club was established in 1862 by fifteen of the city's wealthiest and most influential men, most of whom had strong ties to England. They desired a private meeting place that would also serve as a location to hold important dinners and dances, so a dining room and grand ballroom were necessary inclusions. At the time, Halifax was a very important port city that served shipping routes between Canada, the United States and Europe. The Halifax Club was an immediate success.

But something drove the first general manager to

commit an atrocious act in 1870, when the club was still in its infancy. One day, quite out of the blue, he walked into the dining room where many members were enjoying some good food and company. He stood before them and got everyone's attention. Then he raised a sharp, long knife high in the air above his head and, without giving anyone time to stop him, thrust the knife into his belly with both hands. He died within seconds, his blood pooling on the floor around his unmoving body. Why he killed himself, no one could say.

Jason Clarke, a recent Halifax Club general manager, didn't see the ghost himself, but he did have many staff members report sightings over the years, including the waitress who saw the chandeliers swinging overhead. Another woman was passing by the cloakroom one evening when her body was overcome by an ice-cold sensation. She was instantly certain that she was in the presence of an evil spirit and a shiver ran down her spine. She ran away in fright and was never comfortable in that area again. Other employees reported to Jason that they felt eerie chills while alone in the building and locking up for the night. Sometimes the cold spots were followed by whispers in the walls and other times those whispers turned into shouts. The worst was when the voices would shout the employee's name, as if the original general manager was trying to bark orders from beyond the grave.

Others believe the building is host to many more lost souls who have wandered over from a nearby cemetery. Many of the bodies recovered from the sinking of the *Titanic* were buried in the city, and there are those who claim that some of the restless souls rise from their graves after nightfall and wander Halifax's streets. The Halifax Club might be one stop on their eternal tour around the city. Whether or not the original general manager escorts these wandering souls — none of them members of the Halifax Club — out of the building before stabbing himself in the dining room for the umpteenth time is unknown.

MANDY LIVES

Quesnel, British Columbia

It seemed like an ordinary, quiet day at the Quesnel & District Museum and Archives when Ruth Stubbs, the museum's curator, was met by an unexpected visitor. Well, two unexpected visitors. Lisa Sorensen, who lived in town, entered Ruth's office and dropped Mandy, an old doll, on her desk with little to no care for the antique. Lisa seemed anxious to be rid of Mandy, and Ruth got the sense that the owner was physically repulsed by the toy. Not that Ruth could blame the other woman for feeling that way; she herself felt uneasy the moment she laid eyes on the doll.

Mandy was a little over half a metre tall and wore a white dress and matching bonnet. Her body was made of stuffed cloth but her face and hands were made of porcelain. It was believed she was made between 1900 and 1920, and time hadn't been kind to her. Her face was severely damaged, including cracks around her right eye and discolouration around her mouth that resembled bruising. She had a realistic appearance that gave some people the impression that Mandy was more a living child — one who had been terribly mistreated — than a doll, with a smile described by many as sinister.

Lisa told Ruth that Mandy had belonged to her grandmother, but she didn't want her daughter playing with the doll. Mandy was starting to disintegrate, and Lisa was concerned her daughter would speed that process up and the doll would be damaged beyond repair. Mandy belonged in a museum.

That wasn't the whole truth, as Ruth would later discover, but for the time being she accepted Mandy and placed the doll in a clear plastic bag. Mandy had to remain sealed for forty-eight hours to ensure that her cloth body wasn't infested by insects. When the rest of the museum staff saw Mandy sealed in the bag they admitted that they felt uncomfortable in her presence, and one woman froze and shouted, "Oh, that doll gives me the creeps!" But Mandy passed the bug test, so the next step before being put on display was to be photographed, a regular part of the process for all artifacts.

The next day, experienced museum photographer Cookie Castle arrived to photograph Mandy. Her boyfriend accompanied her to help with the job. As they picked up Mandy and positioned her for a variety of shots, both Cookie and her boyfriend began to experience an uncomfortable feeling, not unlike the wary, unsettling sensation that had overcome Ruth the day she'd first met the doll. In fact, the longer the shoot went on, the more Cookie began to feel that Mandy was starting to resemble a real baby. Nothing else unusual occurred during the photo shoot, but bizarre events happened later that left everyone involved wondering if Mandy was upset at having her picture taken.

After the photo shoot, Cookie hung the negatives in the darkroom, locked up and left as night was falling. When she returned the next morning, she couldn't believe her eyes. The darkroom was in a state of complete disarray. Items had been thrown around the room and pens and pencils were scattered across the floor. It looked like a small child had had a temper tantrum and trashed the place. She shrugged her shoulders and tidied up, then got to work — she still had a job to do. But as she set to the task of developing Mandy's pictures, Cookie heard a loud sigh right behind her, followed by a bang as if something had fallen off a shelf and landed on the floor. Cookie left the darkroom pale and shaking.

She's not the only photographer who has encountered difficulties while trying to work with Mandy. Ruth invited Ross Mitchell, a photographer for the *Cariboo Observer*, to take a series of photographs of the doll, an opportunity Ross jumped at. When he returned to his office and tried to print contact sheets of the pictures, they never emerged from the developer — they had simply disappeared somewhere inside the machine. As Ross tried to figure out what had happened, he suddenly heard footsteps on the floor directly above. Since he knew he was the only person in the building at the time, he feared that someone had

Mandy the doll

broken in. So he climbed upstairs, ready to call the police, but didn't see another living soul.

Another newspaper photographer, Seth Gotro of the *Quesnel Advocate,* had an even more difficult and creepy experience. When he set up his camera to take Mandy's picture, the doll turned her head away from his lens so he couldn't get a head-on shot. Seth had to request special permission to remove Mandy from her case, and when he sat her on a bed to photograph her, she appeared to grin at him with evil intent every time his flash went off.

Sometime later, Ruth Trussler, a tourist visiting from Calgary, tried to videotape Mandy. Her camera had worked flawlessly throughout the museum, but as soon as Ruth turned it toward the doll she was overcome with the feeling that Mandy didn't want to be captured on film or video. Before

Ruth moved on, her camera began to malfunction. Oddly, it worked fine when she pointed it toward other museum artifacts, away from Mandy. And when Ruth returned home and tried to watch the tape, it became wedged in her VCR. She was never able to view her footage.

Many people claim to have seen Mandy's glass eyes follow them as they pass her. She has been blamed for the disappearance — and later reappearance — of many items belonging to museum staff members. At one time she was kept with other antique dolls but had to be separated and encased in glass, alone except for a small toy lamb that was placed on her lap, since people got the impression she was hurting the other dolls when no one was around. Unfortunately, even locking her in her own case isn't always an effective way to keep her safely contained. One morning the toy lamb was found on the floor next to Mandy's case. The most far-fetched and spine-tingling claim is that one day Mandy was accidentally dropped and real blood poured out the cracks on her head and face.

Curator Ruth Stubbs didn't know what else to do with Mandy, so she turned to a retired curator who was well-known and respected in the field. This man could touch antiques and get a feel for them, often accurately picking up on details about artifacts that others had overlooked. He took Mandy from her case and held her in his large, wrinkled hands for a quiet, tense moment. Then he proclaimed that Mandy had seen a great deal of abuse over the years, and admitted to Ruth that he had been overcome by chills as soon as his skin had touched her porcelain.

Desperately needing to know more about the doll, Ruth

returned to Lisa, the previous owner, to do a little digging. After some prompting, Lisa finally admitted that she hadn't simply donated Mandy out of fear that her daughter would damage her, as she'd originally claimed. The truth was a lot more complicated, and a lot more terrifying. When Lisa had inherited the doll, she had stored Mandy in the basement. Soon after, she heard a baby crying in the middle of the night. The eerie sound was coming from her basement. But when she finally found the courage to head down into the darkness, the crying stopped and Lisa saw that one of the windows was open, the curtain blowing in the breeze. That was odd, since she was certain she hadn't left it open. She closed the window and returned to bed. Then the next night, the exact same thing happened — the baby's cries, the empty basement, the open window. This continued every night until Lisa grew convinced that Mandy was somehow responsible, and she unloaded the doll on the museum curator. At least she found some relief; the very first night that Lisa was free of Mandy, the baby cries stopped, and they never returned.

Lisa also revealed that Mandy had originally belonged to a couple from England with young twin children. Tragically, the twins died of polio. Is it possible that Mandy was possessed by one of the children . . . or maybe even both? We'll probably never know.

Take a deep look into Mandy's scarred face and glass eyes. She — as well as a ghost or two — will look straight back at you.

SOMETHING IN THE WALLS OF VENGEANCE HOUSE

Yarmouth, Nova Scotia

Early morning sunlight filtered into the bedroom and gently woke teenagers Lydia and Maria. Maria had spent the night at Lydia's house — as she often did, since they were best friends and nearly inseparable. Lydia's father, Captain Richan, had served as midshipman on a battle-ship called *Vengeance,* and he'd named his home and inn after the ship. Vengeance House, later known as Richan's Tavern, was built in the late 1700s and was the first inn in Yarmouth. It also served as the original courthouse, jail and council chambers. The large wooden building was therefore always filled with interesting characters with news from afar, which made it an ideal location for Lydia and Maria to spend time together and try to overhear anything exciting that was being discussed. And so it wasn't unusual that the girls' sleepovers were most often in Vengeance House, instead of Maria's nearby home.

As they slowly woke and sat up in bed, rubbing sleep out of their eyes and stretching with a yawn, the girls began discussing what they'd seen and heard in the inn the night before. But their conversation was soon interrupted by a *tap-tap-tap* on the wall above the headboard. A short period of silence followed as the girls stopped talking and listened, but soon it happened again. *Tap-tap-tap.* They assumed it was someone in the inn tapping on the opposite side of the wall, so they paid it little attention and continued talking about the previous night.

But the tapping followed them throughout Vengeance House. Oddly this only occurred when Maria was visiting; when she left, so too did the tapping. When she returned, the *tap-tap-tap* trailed the girls like a wolf tracking prey. While it began to concern and frighten the girls, others in the inn attributed the sound to rats in the walls.

Two weeks later, Captain Richan was in bed while his wife, children and Maria were moving about the house. Although Lydia knew her father was trying to rest, she and Maria were having a lot of fun and had trouble keeping their voices down, laughing and shouting happily. Mrs. Richan yelled at the girls to be quiet, so Lydia suggested to her friend that they go up to her room where they could listen for the tapping again. It sounded like a simple bit of harmless fun, so Maria eagerly agreed and the two of them went upstairs.

They took a candle to light their way and blew it out

once they had both slipped into bed. The tapping began immediately, but it was much faster and louder than ever before. It sounded angry and threatening. *Tap-tap-tap! Tap-tap-tap! Tap-tap-tap!* Not only that, but the sound came from the walls, floor and ceiling — it was all around them, surrounding them, closing in on them. *Tap-tap-tap! Tap-tap-tap! Tap-tap-tap!*

In a blind panic, the girls huddled together in the dark and shouted for Mrs. Richan to bring a light. Suspecting the girls were still horsing around, she shouted up from downstairs for them to stop it immediately or else suffer the consequences. But Lydia and Maria continued to scream for help, and Mrs. Richan realized they were serious — deadly serious. She ran to the room and found her daughter and her friend in hysterics, crying and screaming for their lives, so she called her husband. Captain Richan rushed down the hall, barged into the room and, after being brought up to speed on what had frightened the girls so much, listened intently.

After a moment, he and Mrs. Richan both heard the sinister sound too.

Tap-tap-tap.

It was rats in the walls. It must have been. Without pausing to think of a more sensible way to deal with the rodents he was certain were the cause of the sound, he tracked the tapping to the ceiling and tore a hole in it, exposing the space above. But there were no rats. Worse yet, the tapping continued.

Shortly after, word spread that Vengeance House was haunted by ghosts that went *tap-tap-tap* on the walls.

Curiosity seekers came to Yarmouth from far and wide to listen to the phantoms that lived between rooms in the inn. But a guest who was living in the inn at the time, Captain Neale from Salem, Massachusetts, believed Maria and Lydia had created some sort of elaborate hoax for some unknown reason, and he was determined to uncover what that reason was. Captain Neale was an elderly, religious, intelligent man and he wasn't willing to accept that the tapping was caused by rats or that the girls weren't somehow behind the disturbance. Captain Neale offered a $500 reward — a small fortune in those days — to anyone who could prove how the trick was being done.

Eager to claim the money, many tried to find the cause of the tapping, which still continued whenever Maria visited Lydia. A crowd assembled and sought ways to prove that the girls were creating it. They were instructed to sit on a bench in the middle of the room so that neither their feet nor hands were touching the floor or the walls. After a moment, the tapping began, more loudly and fiercely than the day Captain Richan had torn a hole in the ceiling — it was so loud that everyone present was concerned the walls and ceiling might crack in half. Someone suggested the girls might be knocking on the bench somehow, so they were placed on a pile of feather beds. It had no effect on the tapping, which continued without pause.

Someone else suggested that they try to communicate with the ghosts, so the crowd devised a code that would allow the ghosts to answer some questions. Sensible questions were answered by the ghosts with more tapping, but foolish questions meant to trip up the ghosts were answered with a new sound: ear-splitting scratching, like nails on a chalkboard, that forced everyone to cover their ears. Next, doctors, ministers and lawyers were brought to Vengeance House to ask the ghosts challenging questions that non-professionals would have no way of answering, but the ghosts responded to every single one without making a mistake. There was no explanation for the phenomenon.

A foreign captain was in town waiting for fair weather before setting sail.

"When can I leave?" he asked the ghosts.

No answer.

"Am I going to die?" the captain asked.

There was still no answer.

Growing agitated that the ghosts had hitherto answered — correctly, no less — every single sensible question that had been asked of them but were refusing to answer his, the captain desperately spurted out a series of requests. "How many years will I live? How many months? How many weeks?"

Silence.

With a tremble in his voice, the captain quietly asked, "How many days?"

Tap. Tap. Tap.

The captain chuckled nervously. Surely it was some sort of joke, he thought. But three days later, still waiting to sail, he died suddenly from unknown causes on a Yarmouth street.

The stress caused by the ghosts began to take a grave toll on Maria's physical and mental health. She stopped eating and lost weight rapidly, causing her to fall ill. Her family forbade her to visit Vengeance House again, fearful that spending any more time there would soon kill her. Maria stayed home, and the tapping was never heard again. With time, Maria's health rebounded and she was soon her old self again.

But six months later, Maria was at home talking with her family when she suddenly screamed in fright. Her family panicked and asked what was wrong. Maria jumped off her chair — a snake had twisted around her leg and was slithering along her skin. Maria fainted with terror and the snake uncoiled itself, then slithered to the floor. As it sped across the room, Maria's family heard it make a peculiar sound, a sound they'd never heard a snake make before.

Tap-tap-tap!

And then the tapping snake disappeared beneath an old desk. In an attempt to catch it, the family moved every piece of furniture in the room, but the snake was gone.

Maria eventually recovered, and from that day forward she never heard tapping — not from ghosts or snakes — again.

FOLLOW THE LIGHT

South Melville, Prince Edward Island

There was a chill in the night air as Duncan Matheson travelled west along Green Road. He shivered and clutched his jacket a little tighter, trying to ward off the breeze. It was late October in 1899, and Duncan was headed to see his brother, Robert, who lived in South Melville. Robert was sick and Duncan was overdue for a visit.

Duncan's buggy bounced over the road and Nellie, his horse, snorted now and again. The moon was round and bright in the sky, casting an eerie silver-blue glow on the land. The autumn leaves shimmered and danced in the breeze, rustling as if they were whispering to one another. There were no other people out on the road at that hour, but Duncan heard a fox yelp in the far distance, followed by the hoot of an owl from the top of a nearby tree.

Although Duncan wasn't a superstitious man or easily spooked, an odd sensation washed over him and he became convinced that bad news lay ahead. He couldn't explain the feeling, but it was there all the same, like a weight in his stomach that threatened to pull him down off his buggy.

He tried to brush the bad feeling away and took out his pipe. But before he could light it, something upset Nellie and she shied to the side of the road, nearly tipping the buggy over. Duncan yelled out in alarm, gripped the reins tightly in his fists and brought the horse back under control.

They carried on a little farther down the road and the night was once again silent. There was still no one nearby and no sign of what had upset Nellie, and they travelled on in relative peace, although Duncan's bad feeling was growing bigger. But then Nellie shied to the side of the road again, without warning or any sign of provocation. Duncan settled the horse again and felt his anger starting to flare. Nellie had never acted like that and he was upset that she had nearly thrown him out of the buggy twice in a row.

But his anger was short-lived. A brilliant flash of light filled the air behind him, lighting the road and surrounding woods. Duncan turned around to locate the source of the light and, with a growing sense of fear and trepidation, saw a glowing ball of light hovering in the air far behind. It was roughly the size of a basketball, and much to Duncan's surprise, it flew straight toward him. When it neared the buggy it dipped and passed beneath it, shooting out the other side and passing through Nellie's legs, then hovered above the road before them. This proved too much for Nellie and the horse reared up, whinnied frantically and then landed and kicked her back legs out in fear. She nearly smashed the buggy to pieces. It took Duncan a long time to settle the animal. The ball of light waited patiently ahead of them the entire time. It seemed capable of thought, and Duncan, his attitude toward superstitions beginning to erode, was starting to believe that it was a ghost.

As soon as Nellie and Duncan had settled down, the light began to drift farther down the road, leading them on.

Although Nellie was still agitated and reluctant to move, Duncan was able to lead her forward. They followed the light along Green Road all the way to Robert's farm-house, where it turned off the road, floated down the narrow driveway, and passed through a main-floor window.

Duncan paused. Like before, another grave feeling overcame him, but this one was worse — much, much worse. He didn't know how he knew it, but he was nearly certain that his brother was dead.

With the sensation of dread spreading through his bones and slowing him down, he unhitched the horse and stabled her, then entered the house. Inside was as quiet as a cemetery at midnight. Duncan crossed through the front hall and entered his brother's room, wondering whether or not Robert would be there.

He was, although not how Duncan had hoped. Instead, Duncan found Robert lying corpse-still in a casket.

Robert's family later informed Duncan that Robert had died the night before. Both of his bad feelings had turned out to be true and Duncan was surer than ever that the light that had led him to the house was not only a ghost, but the ghost of his dead brother.

MOVING IN WITH THE DEAD

Saint John, New Brunswick

Bill walked around the small and dated house in the west end of Saint John and decided that, despite the house's shortcomings, it would be fine for the time being. He told the owners, the couple who had just given him the tour of the property, that he'd be happy to rent it.

The owners gave each other an odd sideways glance. After an awkward pause, the man said, "I have to tell you something."

Bill waited patiently for the man to reveal what he and his girlfriend had clearly been putting off sharing. Finally, he told Bill that there was nothing physically wrong with the house — everything was in good working order, despite its age and old-fashioned layout — but that he and his girl-friend were moving out because it was haunted.

Without hesitation Bill said, "That won't bother me."

The man still felt obligated to ensure Bill knew what he was getting himself into. The couple had hired a psychic to visit the house, and the conclusion was that there was no doubt a spirit lurking within the old building. The man and woman had only lived there for a few months and already the constant paranormal activity was too much for them. They couldn't bear the thought of spending another night in the house.

Bill still wasn't disturbed. "Hey," he said. "I don't believe in ghosts."

Despite his skepticism, he'd soon wish he'd reconsidered before signing the rental agreement.

Before he officially moved in, Bill visited the house a few times and did a lot of cleaning. The house was pretty messy and it looked a lot better when he'd finished sprucing it up. Bill had spent a lot of time working in Europe and had moved to New Brunswick to work some odd jobs, with the goal of opening his own business. If that happened he'd move out of the rental house and buy his own place, but now that he'd done some cleaning and minor repairs, he felt better about his new accommodations. That happy feeling changed the very first day he moved in.

It started slowly. He'd hear odd noises from different parts of the house, noises he couldn't identify or explain. Small items and personal belongings would move from room to room on their own. Bill kept his tape recorder on the dining room table to listen to music, but as soon as he'd leave the room someone would start messing with the volume — either turning it down so low he could barely hear it or cranking it up so loud it hurt his ears.

Bill was starting to wonder if the couple had been correct in their assessment of the property.

One day when he left the dining room and entered the kitchen the music's volume once again turned up and down. So Bill stood in the doorway between the two rooms and shouted, "Stop that fooling around with my tape deck!"

The ghost didn't appreciate being scolded.

The kitchen cabinet nearest Bill started violently swinging open and shut, open and shut, open and shut. It went *bang, bang, bang!* And every time it opened it nearly hit Bill in the head, as if the ghost was trying not only to frighten him, but to injure him.

After that scary episode, Bill became a believer. And the paranormal activity continued.

Late one night as Bill went upstairs to bed, he finally identified the eerie sound he'd heard when he moved in. It was the hiss of flowing oxygen and it reminded Bill of the sounds you hear in a hospital. But he still couldn't find the source of the sound. Sometimes he'd wake up in the middle of the night and hear someone coughing. Footsteps regularly passed through the house when he was all alone.

Peculiar items that didn't belong to Bill began to appear in odd places. He found a woman's earring on the side of his bathroom sink, grubby picture hooks and tacks on the dining room table and a brass dinner bell beside the kitchen sink.

One day Bill placed his vacuum cleaner in the family room, then sat down on the couch because something on

TV had caught his attention. A bit of time passed and Bill decided to go to the kitchen to get some lunch. As soon as he left the family room the vacuum cleaner turned on and started cleaning the floor all on its own.

"Stop it!" Bill yelled in a panic.

This time the ghost listened and the vacuum cleaner turned off.

In search of an explanation for the nightmare he'd knowingly moved into, Bill began asking everyone and anyone if they knew anything about the house's history. A man he'd hired to upgrade the kitchen counters happened to have a strong connection to the house. He'd been a pallbearer at the funeral of the woman who had previously lived there. Her name was Marion, and the contractor told him there had been some sort of friction between her and the rest of her family. She'd died in the house long ago, and her death was neither peaceful nor quick. She'd suffered for a long time before she passed, and had needed to be watched at all hours since she was constantly coughing and choking.

The news sent shivers down Bill's spine. What the contractor had revealed lined up with the noises he'd heard and the items that had appeared throughout the house. He knew that he was sharing the home with Marion.

Bill was having second thoughts about moving in, and was considering moving out and starting over somewhere else. But then he made a fortunate discovery.

During his time in Europe he had picked up the habit of buying flowers in order to brighten up his home. He even bought flowers to make hotel rooms cheerier. One day in Saint John he decided to resume this custom and he purchased some flowers for the dining room table.

The ghostly disturbances stopped immediately.

It then dawned on Bill that there were plenty of old vases left behind throughout the house, and he later found growing lights in the basement. These discoveries, coupled with the fact that the spirit seemed to be much happier once he started filling the house with fresh-cut flowers on a regular basis, led him to believe that Marion had been an avid gardener and loved plants.

In the days that followed, Bill would still occasionally hear Marion walking about the house, but he wasn't attacked again the way he had been when he scolded her in the kitchen. Over time he grew accustomed to living with a ghost and he continued to buy flowers to keep her happy. But Bill believed that Marion had remained there for a reason, since she had such a strong presence and was quick to fly off the handle. What the purpose was, Bill could never say. Perhaps a future tenant will discover the ghost's true intent, for as long as the house stands, Marion will haunt it.

THE BODY IN THE BROOK

Chester, Nova Scotia

It had been an extremely damp and cold winter in the town of Chester one year during the early part of the nineteenth century. The townsfolk were eager for spring to arrive so they could enjoy more time outdoors in the sun. The snow melted, the leaves blossomed on the trees and the air was once again filled with birdsong. As soon as it was warm enough for a swim, a group of young boys raced through town with their swimsuits on, laughing and smiling. They crossed the bridge on Victoria Street, peeled off their shirts and tossed them forgotten to the ground, then ran straight into Back Harbour without slowing down. The water was still frigid and the boys shrieked in shock, but their bodies soon got used to the cold. Before long one of the more daring, adventurous boys ventured a little

Chester's Old Stone Bridge

farther away from the others. He soon wished he hadn't.

As the boy was treading water and urging his friends to follow him, a bloated, waterlogged body broke the surface beside him. The man's skin was an odd greenish-bronze colour, and much of his flesh had peeled away. His mouth was wide open in a silent scream. The boy's scream, on the other hand, could have woken the dead. And when the other boys saw what was wrong, they added their own voices to the fray.

The townsfolk were quick to rush to the scene of the commotion as the boys hurriedly swam back to dry land. The body was carefully removed from the water and was identified as a man named Mr. Brown from Annapolis Valley. Mr. Brown had travelled to Chester the previous winter and had vanished without a trace. After it surfaced in the spring, his body was returned to Annapolis Valley to receive a proper burial, but his spirit remained.

In the years that followed, the wooden bridge that crossed Back Harbour and the Old Mill Race Stream developed a bad reputation. Late at night, long after the sun had set and the air took on a chill, people saw what looked like a white shadow — perhaps fog — drift out of the harbour and slowly climb up the side of the bridge. It moved with purpose, however, so it couldn't simply be shadow and fog. And when late-night travellers squinted their eyes and moved closer for a better look, they discovered with a sense of shock that it was actually a man — a man who looked just like the deceased Mr. Brown — and that he was climbing the bridge as if trying to escape his watery grave. Where the ghost of Mr. Brown went and what he did once he reached the top of the bridge no living soul could say. Even the biggest and bravest men and women fled in terror at the sight of the ghost climbing out of the harbour, and most horses refused to cross the bridge any time of day, perhaps sensing that something bad had happened there.

The wooden bridge was destroyed during a bad storm known as the Saxby Gale in 1869, and it might have been expected that the ghost of Mr. Brown would move on, but he was not so easily set aside. When a new stone bridge was constructed around 1882, locals and travellers once again began witnessing the ghost emerge from the water and climb up the side of the bridge late at night. People learned that it was best to cross in the dead centre of the bridge (if they had to cross at all) in order to avoid the sides and what might jump over the edge at any moment.

Why is the ghost so determined to remain in Chester, frightening the townsfolk with each setting sun? A rumour circulated among the locals shortly after Mr. Brown's body surfaced from the bottom of the harbour. It was said that the night he'd disappeared, Mr. Brown had visited a small inn that once stood near the bridge. Mrs. Mallack, the old woman who ran the less-than-savoury establishment, made sure there was no shortage of beer and rum at all times, and she allowed her patrons to gamble until the early hours of the morning. Mr. Brown joined a game with a group of local men and was doing quite well when one of the men accused him of cheating. Without affording Mr. Brown the opportunity to defend himself against the claim, the man pulled out a gun and shot Mr. Brown where he sat, killing him instantly.

A dead silence filled the inn as the grim reality of what had just happened gripped the small crowd, and Mr. Brown's blood pooled around his lifeless body on the floor. They couldn't bury the body since the ground was frozen, so they dragged it under cover of darkness to the bridge and dumped it over the edge, where it fell into the harbour. Everyone involved promised never to speak of the night's events again, but they never could have guessed that Mr. Brown's ghost would return.

In 1902 Gail Smith's grandparents bought the inn and turned it into their home. The Smiths passed the story of Mr. Brown's murder down from one generation to the next, and Gail recalls her father sharing all the gory details with her when she was young. One of the more unnerving details was that Mrs. Mallack had allegedly tried to cover up the murder by scrubbing the dining room floor as well as she could, and painting the floors to hide the remaining blood stain. Gail had no idea at the time how accurate this story was, but when the house was torn down in 1958 she made a startling discovery. Upon examining a piece of the original flooring from the dining room, Gail clearly saw, hidden under a layer of chipped paint, the dark red stains of Mr. Brown's blood soaked into the hardwood.

From that day on, Gail never again doubted the story she'd been told as a child. And the townsfolk of Chester — at least those who also know the story — steer clear of the haunted stone bridge.

TO DIE IN DURHAM

Whitby, Ontario

It was late at night and the only sounds in the building came from a set designer's tools. He was constructing a set in the Centennial Building, a large community theatre in downtown Whitby that originally served as the Ontario County Courthouse in Durham region. The man was on the stage working when he suddenly had the distinct impression that he was being watched. He jerked his head up and spotted a man standing at the edge of the second-floor balcony.

"Hello," the set designer called out.

The man on the balcony didn't answer. He was dressed in old-fashioned clothing: a white ruffled shirt with black pants and a dark hat. He might have been an actor, except the clothes didn't match the current production's costumes.

The proof that the man wasn't a member of the theatre's cast or crew — in fact, that he wasn't a part of the living world at all — came when he stepped off the edge of the balcony and floated effortlessly to the ground. He then walked along the centre aisle between the theatre's seats, glided up onto the stage and stared at the set designer, who couldn't believe his eyes (the mystery man, he could now see, was translucent), and finally turned and disappeared through the side door.

Stephen Welling and Shirley Richard have a theory about who the ghost — who is often seen falling or jumping off the balcony — is, and why he can't leave the building. They were invited to join a *Whitby This Week* newspaper reporter and photographer, as well as a custodian who worked there, to spend the night in the Centennial Building in an attempt to figure out who the man might be. Stephen and Shirley were well-known psychics, and as they sat on the stage with the other three people, they picked up on a possible explanation. They both felt that in the 1800s a youth was on trial where the stage now stands, while an older man — possibly the youth's father or uncle — was pacing nervously in the balcony. When the judge passed a guilty verdict, the man, distraught and irrational, ran to the edge of the railing to protest and accidentally tumbled over and fell to his death.

The case that the psychics picked up on does match a couple of trials that were held in the courthouse in the late 1800s, but other people believe the ghost might belong to one of the two men tried in the building and hanged at the nearby Ontario County Jail in 1910 and 1946,

The Ontario County Courthouse, around 1895

respectively. But if that's the case, it doesn't explain the earliest report of a ghost haunting the building, which dates back to 1873.

An article that appeared in the *Whitby Chronicle* that year described the ghost as the "talk of the town." A crowd gathered at the courthouse on July 30, hoping to catch a glimpse of the spirit. Rumours had spread through the community that the building was haunted, and that the ghost had been spotted in different forms. Some had heard the most sorrowful moaning before the ghost appeared, setting their hair on end. At times the ghost was that of a man leaning on a staff by the front door, and other times walking back and forth from the front steps to the gate during the witching hour, stopping occasionally to look up at the sky and groan as if in great physical and emotional pain. When approached, the man would burst into flames and sink into the ground. Scarier still, he'd also been caught transforming into a large black dog with burning red eyes.

One caretaker who used to work there often brought his dog to keep him company. Turns out even if the caretaker had left his dog at home he wouldn't have been alone. The dog would often bolt to the balcony and sniff around excitedly, then wag his tail as if some unseen presence was standing there. And the building's lights would quite regularly flicker on their own, making anyone brave enough to be alone wish they were anywhere but inside the old courthouse.

These days, the most tragic drama in the Centennial Building might not be taking place on the stage, but among the spectators on the balcony.

SECRET ROOM

Hudson, Quebec

Things might have turned out much better — or differently, at least — for sisters Kyle and Lindsay if their parents had never discovered the secret room.

The family moved into Riverwood, a large house built around the turn of the twentieth century on the south bank of the Ottawa River, in 1963. One warm summer day, the girls' father was cleaning the second-storey windows from inside the house while their mother was gardening outside. The mother took a short break and walked around the perimeter of the house, enjoying the natural beauty of the family's new property while surveying her husband's work. Sunlight reflected brightly off the freshly cleaned windows, but then she noticed one that didn't appear to have been touched. The window was covered in dirt and old, tangled cobwebs.

"You missed the round window," she told her husband when she found him inside.

He didn't know what she was talking about. Not only had he methodically gone room to room cleaning each and every window on the second floor, but he wasn't even aware of the window his wife was talking about. It didn't exist — at least, not to his knowledge. But she insisted that there was a round window and he had somehow missed it.

They walked outside and around the house. Sure enough, at the back of the house there was a round window and it clearly hadn't been cleaned in a long, long time. But neither parent could think how to get to that particular window from inside the house. It was almost as if it existed on the outside of the house only.

They walked upstairs and guessed that the window must be behind a wall near the back staircase. They rapped on the wall and realized that their knocks sounded hollower than they should. After giving the matter a little further thought, they decided to break through the bathroom wall to see what — if anything — was hidden on the other side. They never could have guessed what they'd find.

Having used a sledgehammer to break a hole in the wall large enough to step through, the parents were amazed to find a secret room that had been sealed off from the rest of the house some time ago. It was very large with a high ceiling, and had empty shelves and cubbyholes. The room might have been used as a storage closet for the maid who at one time lived in Riverwood, but no one could figure out why it had been sealed up and forgotten. It was as if a previous owner wanted to hide the room, or forget it was there. But now that the parents had discovered it they decided to affix a door to the hole they'd created and turn it into the mother's sewing room.

That's when bad things started happening.

Lindsay and Kyle felt an evil presence inside, particularly upstairs near the secret room. The air would suddenly and unexpectedly grow very cold and dark, and one of their two younger brothers, who was only five years old at the time, told his sisters that he heard things moving in his room in the middle of the night. He'd often wake up to find that his dressers, which were far too heavy for him to lift, had been dragged across the room.

Lindsay and Kyle shared a bedroom, and one night an unusual and eerie sound woke Lindsay. They sat up in their beds and, after realizing that neither girl was dreaming, watched in mute horror as their closet door slowly slid open. Then someone pulled the string that turned on the hanging lightbulb with a sharp *click-click* sound. Both the bulb and the string swayed side to side in the air, but the girls could clearly see in the light that no one was in the closet. But *something* was in there, and whatever it was didn't like the way the clothes were arranged. The unseen presence began sliding the girls' clothes frantically from side to side, then took dresses off the closet rod and placed them back in different positions.

"Are you awake?" Lindsay whispered.

"Yes," Kyle responded.

"Are you seeing this?"

"Yes!"

Hearing her sister's terrified voice in the dark and knowing that she was also watching the activity in the closet made it more horribly real for Lindsay. The ordeal lasted for thirty minutes.

When they needed to go to the bathroom in the middle of the night, all four of the children often saw a small blue light travelling down the hallway just in front of them. The light would sometimes move in an erratic pattern and other times bounce through the air. The girls came to think of it as "Tinkerbell." The light would pass under a thick curtain that hung across the hallway, and when the children pulled the curtain to the side they would see the light pass beneath the door of the bathroom — the same bathroom where their parents had created a doorway to the secret room. But when the children entered the bathroom the light would be gone. Despite the fact that they all saw the light on many separate occasions, none of the children discussed it with each other until they were much older.

As creepy as the paranormal activity in Riverwood had been, it was about to become much, much worse.

Lindsay returned home after school one bright, sunny winter day and entered her bedroom. She stopped dead in her tracks and screamed at the top of her lungs. In the centre of a large, ornate mirror on the wall was a brass lion sculpture. It was glaring out at her from within the mirror with a look of intense hatred. Kyle rushed to Lindsay's side and asked what was wrong, but when Kyle looked at the mirror all she saw was her own reflection, her sister's and the rest of the room.

Lindsay and Kyle outside of Riverwood

The lion appeared in the same mirror again and again throughout the winter, and finally Kyle saw it too. Being a brass statue, it never moved while the girls looked at it, but every time it appeared it wore a different expression. The one consistency was that its expression was always angry, mean and scary looking. Then, six months later, the lion stopped appearing in the mirror.

Late one night the following winter, one of the girls woke up with a bad feeling in her gut and immediately roused her sister. Outside their bedroom window were two red eyes staring in at them. All they could see were the eyes — the person's (or creature's) body was hidden in the darkness of the night. And whatever was out there looking in at them was somehow floating in the air, for there was nowhere to stand and nothing to hold on to outside that particular window. The red eyes — the sisters came to think of them as "devil's eyes" — appeared four more times that winter, either in the middle of the night or at twilight.

The family moved out of Riverwood in 1968, but they could never forget about the old home. Haunted houses have a tendency to haunt their occupants for the rest of their lives, long after the terrifying events are distant memories.

PHOTO CREDITS

Page 4: Courtesy of Milena Rzepa Sztainbok
Pages 16–17: Queen's University Archives, Kingston Picture Collection, Locator #V23, Cem-Fron-7
Page 28: Murray Lundberg
Page 33: Courtesy Town of Stony Plain
Page 36: Susan Mcarthur Letellier/Dreamstime
Page 46: Shawn Edlund/Dreamstime
Page 59: County of Oxford Archives
Page 64: Shankar S/Flickr
Page 83: Quesnel & District Museum and Archives
Page 102: Courtesy of Kevin Barrett, Nova Scotia Communities, Culture & Heritage Department
Page 108: Whitby Public Library Archives Image 07-001-005
Page 114: Courtesy of Lindsay Damecour

Joel A. Sutherland is an author and librarian. He is the author of several books in the Haunted Canada series, as well as *Be a Writing Superstar, Summer's End* and Haunted, a series of middle-grade horror novels. His short fiction has appeared in many anthologies and magazines, alongside the likes of Stephen King and Neil Gaiman. He has been a juror for the John Spray Mystery Award and the Monica Hughes Award for Science Fiction and Fantasy.

He appeared as "The Barbarian Librarian" on the Canadian edition of the hit television show *Wipeout,* making it all the way to the third round and proving that librarians can be just as tough and crazy as anyone else.

Joel lives with his family in southeastern Ontario, where he is always on the lookout for ghosts.

HAUNTED CANADA

Read the whole chilling series.

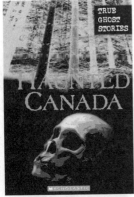

978-0-7791-1410-8

978-0-439-96122-6

978-0-439-93777-1

978-1-4431-2893-3

978-1-4431-3929-8

978-1-4431-4878-8

978-1-4431-4881-8

For Haunted Canada bonus material,
visit www.scholastic.ca/hauntedcanada.